The First Letter of Peter

The First Letter of Peter

A Global Commentary

Edited by Jennifer Strawbridge
Contributions by members of
the St Augustine Seminar

scm press

© The Lambeth Conference Ltd 2020

Published in 2020 by SCM Press
Editorial office
3rd Floor, Invicta House,
108–114 Golden Lane,
London EC1Y 0TG, UK
www.scmpress.co.uk

Second impression 2020

SCM Press is an imprint of Hymns Ancient & Modern Ltd
(a registered charity)

Hymns Ancient & Modern® is a registered trademark of
Hymns Ancient & Modern Ltd
13A Hellesdon Park Road, Norwich,
Norfolk NR6 5DR, UK

Scripture quotations are from New Revised Standard Version
Bible: Anglicized Edition, copyright © 1989, 1995 National
Council of the Churches of Christ in the United States of
America. Used by permission. All rights reserved worldwide.

British Library Cataloguing in Publication data

A catalogue record for this book is available
from the British Library

978-0-334-05887-8

Typeset by Regent Typesetting
Printed and bound by
CPI Group (UK) Ltd

Contents

About the Editor and Contributors

Editor

Jennifer Strawbridge, Associate Professor in New Testament Studies, University of Oxford.

Contributors and authors from the St Augustine Seminar

Margaret Aymer, First Presbyterian Church Shreveport, D. Thomason Professor of New Testament, Austin Presbyterian Seminary.

Markus Bockmuehl, Dean Ireland's Professor in the Exegesis of Holy Scripture, University of Oxford.

Ian Boxall, Associate Professor of New Testament, The Catholic University of America.

Christopher Brittain, Dean of Divinity and Margaret E. Fleck Chair in Anglican Studies, Trinity College, University of Toronto.

Chris Chivers, Principal of Westcott House, Cambridge.

Ani Ghazaryan Drissi, Faculty of Theology, University of Geneva; Programme Executive for the World Council of Churches Faith and Order Commission.

Musa Dube, Professor of Theology and Religious Studies, University of Botswana.

Jeremy Duff, Principal of the St Padarn's Institute, The Church in Wales.

Maurice Elliott, Director of the Church of Ireland Theological Institute.

Paula Gooder, Canon Chancellor, St Paul's Cathedral, London.

Isabelle Hamley, Chaplain to the Archbishop of Canterbury.

Christopher M. Hays, Professor of New Testament, Fundación Universitaria Seminario Biblico de Colombia.

Robert Heaney, Director of the Center for Anglican Communion Studies, Virginia Theological Seminary.

Wesley Hill, Associate Professor of New Testament, Trinity School for Ministry.

ABOUT THE EDITOR AND CONTRIBUTORS

Josiah Idowu-Fearon, General Secretary of the Anglican Communion.

Emma Ineson, Bishop of Penrith.

Craig Keener, F.M. and Ada Thompson Professor of the New Testament, Asbury Theological Seminary.

Hannah Lewis, Pioneer Minister with the Deaf Community, Diocese of Liverpool, and Tutor, All Saints Centre for Mission and Ministry.

Gloria Lita Mapangdol, President and Dean of St Andrew's Theological Seminary, Quezon City.

David Monteith, Dean of Leicester.

Esther Mombo, Associate Professor in the Faculty of Theology, St Paul's University, Limuru.

Cathrine Ngangira, Cranmer Hall.

Kwok Pui Lan, Distinguished Visiting Professor of Theology, Candler School of Theology, Emory University.

Ephraim Radner, Professor of Historical Theology, Wycliffe College.

Amy Richter, The College of the Transfiguration, Grahamstown.

Samy Shehata, Principal of Alexandria School of Theology and Area Bishop at North Africa.

Katherine Sonderegger, William Meade Chair in Systematic Theology, Virginia Theological Seminary.

Stephen Spencer, Director for Theological Education in the Anglican Communion.

Paul Swarup, Presbyter in Charge of Cathedral Church of the Redemption. Vidyaiyothi College of Theology, Delhi.

Jennifer Strawbridge, Associate Professor of New Testament Studies, University of Oxford.

Yak-hwee Tan, Associate Professor of Biblical Studies, Tainan Theological College.

Paulo Ueti, Theological Advisor and Regional Facilitator for Latin America of the Anglican Alliance; Assistant Director for Theological Education in the Anglican Communion for Portuguese, Spanish and French speaking regions.

Caroline Welby, International Retreat Leader.

Gerald West, Professor of Biblical Studies at University of KwaZulu-Natal.

Robyn Whitaker, Senior Lecturer in New Testament, Pilgrim Theological College, University of Divinity, Australia.

Foreword

by the Most Revd Justin Welby, Archbishop of Canterbury

Scripture reveals divine truth and thus changes people. In all its remarkable diversity it penetrates deep into the heart of readers and their societies. Peter's First Letter will change people, as it has always transformed those who have read it. They have found that it has spoken to their experience of Christian life and community. They have struggled with its ideas, argued with its content – not least on the roles of men, women and slaves, as well as attitudes to government. Above all, people have quoted it: 'love covers a multitude of sins' and 'the word of the Lord endures for ever'.

Peter addresses a people who are suffering or fearing that they will suffer for their faith. He points them towards God's view of the dramatic, earth-shaking, soul-transforming change that comes through following Christ; to the before and after of conversion, to hope that gives resilience, and to the consequences of being God's holy people. Following Christ is not a passive and private affair, to be conducted in secrecy and shame, but a call of all to mutual love, unity of spirit, compassion, and above all to give glory to Christ and draw people to faith, despite difference and suffering. Christians, Peter tells us, should be different; exiles and strangers marked apart by hope, by holiness, by their love for their neighbour, one another and Jesus Christ.

Peter grounds this vision of what it means to suffer for Christ, and to be an alien and exile in this world, in his focus on the 'then' and the 'now'. The theme of then and now is found in the shift from division to reconciliation, from anxiety to humility, from death to life. Once you were not a people, Peter writes, but now you are God's people (1 Peter 2.10). The message of 1 Peter is clear: 'God has created us, changed us, and transformed us into His own people so that as we declare the wonderful works of Him who brought us out of darkness into His marvellous light' (2.9). We too can be instruments of transformation in the world around us.

Living as God's people has consequences for God's church, for our behaviour both towards one another and towards God's world. No church is obedient to God if it focuses only on itself; the focus must be on its mission. The Church must look outward, must engage those who are alien and strange to us, and must be made up of what Peter calls 'living stones', stones that are alive, changed by contact with one another and above all by the work of the Spirit.

The First Letter of Peter is a text for a global church engaging with diversity of culture and attitudes in a twenty-first century that makes possible communication without true relationship. It speaks just as clearly to what it means to be a Christian today as it did to Christians in the first century. It is a letter that, as you will see in what follows, deals with issues of persecution and suffering, of exile and alienation. It is a letter that emphasizes themes of holiness, hope and prayer, with a call to reconciliation and confident witness to the world around us. It is a letter that instructs the people of God that they must seek to live and to lead in a way that shows others that they are God's people, under the authority of Scripture, faithful to Christ and inspired by the Spirit.

It is my hope and prayer that we might be challenged to consider the questions that 1 Peter asks of all of us together as a people of God. As we seek to know better Christ who understands intimately our suffering, our alienation and our division through the agony of his crucifixion, I hope that those at the Lambeth Conference 2020, as well as Christians around the world, will know ever better the loving power, the reconciliation and the salvation that arises through his resurrection. Peter will draw our eyes firmly to Jesus, and to the joy and hope we find in the revelation of his love for us.

It should also send us out as God's church for God's world, a church united, but not unanimous.

This commentary emerges from a group of people, drawn together from across the Anglican Communion and global church, who sought the guidance of the Spirit, wrestled with the Scriptures, and opened themselves to seeing how others encounter the First Letter of Peter. In their openness, honesty and prayer, they sought to strip away the crust of piety so that the Scripture could confront them. They listened to the wisdom of the church through the ages, and to the wisdom of the church throughout the world. The fruit of their work invites others, and invites you, into this same task. You are invited in this commentary to be confronted by Scripture, to lift your vision outward, and to see that God is calling you and your community as God's new people to the business of changing the world and bringing the transforming love of Jesus Christ across the globe.

The Most Revd Justin Welby
Archbishop of Canterbury

Introduction to the Commentary

The transforming joy of Jesus Christ changes lives and communities. The First Letter of Peter is written to communities across Asia Minor who, sanctified by the Spirit, are called to witness to this transforming joy even as they suffer for the name of Christ. Written to a persecuted community, 1 Peter speaks of the struggle of early followers of Jesus to maintain their mission and sense of cohesion in the face of opposition (Elliott 1992, p. 274). The letter offers encouragement for unity over division and for humility over anxiety as it instructs those suffering for their faith in how to live faithfully in the time between Jesus' death and resurrection and his return. It addresses and encourages all who follow Christ, while also engaging specific issues faced by those members of the community who are enslaved, those who are exiles and resident aliens, those who live under human institutions of hierarchy and patriarchy and all who are called to welcome and love the stranger. Across the chapters of 1 Peter, the driving message for all is the transforming joy of faith in Jesus Christ and a call to witness, to hope and to holiness as God's chosen people.

This commentary draws together numerous voices from across the global church in preparation for the Lambeth Conference 2020, the gathering of all Anglican bishops from across the Anglican Communion that takes place once every 10–12 years. Over the course of five days and two meetings in London as well as countless emails and correspondence, faithful scholars from around the world gathered together for the St Augustine Seminar to spend time with 1 Peter and to seek the guidance of the Holy Spirit in their engagement with Scripture. This commentary draws on the stories, struggles and prayers of scholars from six continents and represents a range of Christian traditions and experiences. The work from these gatherings is drawn together in what follows, where different approaches to Scripture are brought together in such a way that difference is not hidden, and the conversation continues. Our hope and prayer is that this commentary invites you and your community to continue this conversation and to experience the transforming love of Christ proclaimed in 1 Peter.

The tone of the commentary is intentionally conversational and even homiletical in places, offering a close reading of 1 Peter and drawing out a number of foundational themes for the Christian community as set forth by its apostolic author: hope, holiness, witness, suffering, joy, hospitality, exile, leadership, resurrection. Across this commentary these themes emerge time and again, with short excursuses woven into each chapter to engage more deeply with the themes and with the text. The five chapters of the commentary mirror the five chapters of 1 Peter, though detailed notes are given in Chapters 2 and 3 for why the chapter divisions of 1 Peter (added after the letter was composed) are not always helpful. This is especially the case in 1 Peter 2 and 3, where the call to various sectors of the Church to 'accept the authority of' (2.13, 18; 3.1) belong together as Peter engages with what it means to acknowledge authority, to submit, to honour and how to return good for evil as a pattern that instructs all Christians in conformity to Christ.

The letter is written to those who are experiencing alienation and suffering. Nevertheless, the people addressed have not been forcibly displaced but rather are part of the diaspora because they have been called into communion by God and are therefore separated from the world, and sometimes from their own social or political communities. This focus leads to a number of interpretations of the text – as the St Augustine Seminar encountered on a small scale – since some will immediately identify with the context of persecution and suffering, and others will not. Importantly, we cannot interpret someone else's suffering for them. Peter's letter not only offers encouragement for those living in difficult times, but also calls others to stand in solidarity with those who are suffering and not in judgement. The letter makes clear that those who are vulnerable don't always have the luxury of resisting oppression or stepping away from suffering, continually returning to the person of Christ and his rejection, unjust suffering and exaltation.

Themes of hope and of holiness are as central to this letter as those of suffering and offer mechanisms for remaining resilient in the face of suffering and, at times, resisting oppressive systems. This move can be found clearly in the strong outsider-insider language found in 1 Peter, where those who call themselves 'Christian' are considered both exiles and aliens, as well as a chosen people, a royal priesthood, a holy nation and God's own people (2.9). The identity of exiles, of those excluded, of those who are suffering, as God's chosen people is subversive. God chose those who were homeless, those who did not belong, those who were deemed outsiders and strangers and made them God's own people, called to holiness. Thus, the text offers hope for those in ambiguous, difficult situations.

Reorientation as God's chosen, holy people doesn't necessarily lead to an escape from suffering, but it does mean that the powers that tried to control, that tried to dominate through fear, can no longer determine who and whose we are. Such a shift is modelled on Christ himself, the suffering servant (as 1 Peter, a letter deeply conversant with Hebrew scriptures, is clear). Hope comes not from the activities, postures or identities we generate on our own, it comes from our following Christ and participation in what God in Christ has initiated.

Accompanying this hope is an unfolding theology of holiness throughout 1 Peter which points to a faith that is dynamic and is deeply connected with the profound holiness of God into which readers are invited (Be holy for God is holy; 1 Peter 1.16). In the context of holiness and suffering, both of which are connected to God in Christ, 1 Peter raises issues for the Church today about how we engage with difference. Most significantly for those who are in communion with Christ, 1 Peter challenges all to reflect on the way we treat each other today and the way we have treated one another in the past. It calls for a transformed behaviour towards each other and the world, one which is focused more on coming together (being built up together as living stones; 1 Peter 2.4–5) than on disagreement. Living a life that is holy is not simply abstention from what is bad, but an imitation of God in the self-sacrificial movement towards the other, imitating God's movement towards us. And thus, 1 Peter speaks of redemption in the midst of conflict and the actions we are called to embody in our world in love.

Within this context, reading 1 Peter opens up a number of challenges for the Church today which are expanded upon throughout this commentary. Such challenges, which can inform our prayer and conversations, include:

- 1 Peter is written to a people who are a minority, scattered in the world, which is an identity that characterizes the Christian life for the apostolic author and his readers: does this identity characterize the Christian life and mission for us today?
- As a letter addressed to people who are powerless, suffering and in situations where they have little choice, what does it mean to do right in those situations? What does it mean to imitate Christ in those situations?
- 1 Peter calls its readers to sanctify Christ as Lord (1 Peter 3.15), not the government (the emperor), not the master, not the husband. These three are introduced as ruling powers embedded within the ancient world, but 1 Peter asks: what might it look like if Jesus is Lord and not the emperor, master, husband?
- Power imbalances are real in 1 Peter and the world today and misuses of power are dangerous, especially when those in power are not always aware they are misusing it. This letter challenges abuse of power – cutting across place and titles, and including abuses that are physical, sexual, economic, authoritarian. Where have inequalities of power led to abuses in the past? Where do they continue to do so and how might all who exercise leadership and welcome continuously reflect on the power they hold?
- Knowing that fear can all too easily corrupt life together in Christ and imprison or further alienate

individuals and peoples, what does it mean for a community of believers to live in hope and not in fear?

- One of the central challenges of the letter can be found in 1 Peter 3.15–16: how might you be 'ready to make your defence to anyone who demands from you an account of the hope that is in you'? What does it look like to live in a way that prompts such questions about Christian hope?

- When making a defence of hope in us, we must ask: what is the Church known for? In many parts of the world it is known for abuse, for infighting, or for disagreements about sexuality. Where is the Church glorifying God? What is the account that the Church and followers of Jesus give for their hope and faith?

- The letter ends with a call to leadership, with Peter including himself among those who are elders in the Church, shepherding a given flock. Such images suggest that openness, fluidity, creativity cannot be detached from the suffering of God's people and the glory that is to come. Where has our ministry lost creativity, openness and connection to those most vulnerable? Where is our ministry most creative and open to exploring new fields and pastures?

In the midst of these challenges, the call to holiness and to conform to Christ found throughout 1 Peter remains. And such a call forms the foundation for seeing this letter as a tapestry, where holiness and following Christ are woven together with joy, suffering, hope, witness and redemption, which we hope you will find in what follows.

This commentary makes up part of the preparatory materials for the Lambeth Conference 2020. However, it is intended for all those who wish to engage in deeper biblical study of 1 Peter, as individuals and as a community. The voices within this commentary are many, emerging from days of dialogue and prayer together in November 2018 and May 2019. Immense gratitude is due to the St Augustine's Foundation – a registered charity that provides grants to support the work of theological education across the Anglican Communion – whose generous grant enabled the preparatory gatherings and production of these materials.

One of the great glories of the Anglican Communion – indeed, of the global church – is that we are sisters and brothers of different ages and backgrounds, spread across so many cultures and contexts. This brings great strength, but also means it is easy for us to misunderstand each other, often not because we are saying something different but because we say it in a different way. We found this at the St Augustine Seminar – we had to listen carefully to each other, to hear each other's valuable insights when expressed in unfamiliar language. We expect that every reader will be disturbed at times by this book, as they read exegesis and interpretation which expresses an unfamiliar or even an unwelcome perspective. At those times, we would encourage you not to get frustrated or angry, but to pray that God would give you wisdom, insight and peace. Often God uses the stranger to reveal himself, his love and his purposes to us. As you encounter the text of 1 Peter, we pray that you may do so with a spirit of curiosity and openness as you seek to discover what the Holy Spirit might say and speak to you through this Scripture.

Introduction to 1 Peter

The First Letter of Peter presents itself as a letter written by 'Peter, an apostle of Jesus Christ' (1.1). The letter portrays its apostolic author in Rome (called Babylon in this letter) and writing in the company of Mark and Silvanus (5.12–13), either or both of whom might be his assistant or indeed ghostwriter. Regardless of authorship 1 Peter is, in subtle but significant respects, deliberately cast in character (Bockmuehl 2012b, pp.142–7).

1 Peter is both embedded in the early Christian movement and deeply conversant with the Hebrew scriptures (for example, 1.24; 2.6–10; 3.10–12), drawing on a number of Jewish and Christian themes and texts. As such, it is understood by scholars to be an ecumenical bridge and anchor. It is called a 'catholic epistle', where catholic means 'universal' since it is addressed to more than one community (which is essential to keep in mind when this commentary speaks of Peter's 'community'). The letter is also connected with more strands of the New Testament than any other letter within it.

Jesus' life and death in 1 Peter resonates with that in the Synoptic tradition (Mark, Matthew and Luke), and elements of this letter echo the writings of the apostle Paul.

The letter is written to Christians in Pontus, Galatia, Cappadocia, Asia and Bithynia, all provinces of the Roman Empire in Asia Minor (modern-day Turkey), and the prescript hints at a prior mission to northern Asia Minor (1.1). These areas are associated with persecution of Christians both here in 1 Peter and in the correspondence in AD 112 of Pliny the Younger with the Emperor Trajan (*Letter* 10.96). The readership is a Christian diaspora – a group of people alienated from the society around them – whom we know to have experienced opposition specifically for their Christian faith and identity (4.12–17). They are suffering as rejected outsiders in their own communities, no longer belonging to a world in which they were once at home (4.1–5). The letter uses a number of powerful metaphors often translated as 'resident alien', 'exile', 'stranger', 'foreigner' and 'sojourner'. This is the context into which Peter speaks his strikingly resonant message of hope and holiness, beginning in the first chapter.

Hope in the midst of persecution is clearly and repeatedly developed as that which unites the readers both with the apostle and with Jesus himself. The description of Jesus' exemplary suffering, including his silence when unjustly abused in his trial (2.23–24), links with the depiction of the death of

Jesus in Synoptic tradition (see Mark 10.45; 14.61; Matt. 20.28) as well as several of Peter's speeches in Acts (see Acts 4.10–12; 10.42–43). Within 1 Peter, the apostolic author encourages Christian leaders as a 'fellow elder' and apostolic 'witness' of Jesus' sufferings (5.1).

1

Called into Hope and Holiness in Christ[1]
(1 Peter 1)

'Life is Short' (2010), Nancy Rourke.

'Life is Short': 1 Peter is addressed 'to the exiles of the Dispersion' (1.1). The word 'exile' contains echoes of outsider, the odd one out, someone who is different. In the deaf resistance art of Nancy Rourke, the figure in a different shade and with a smile (the only one in colour in the original) represents a deaf person who has discovered sign language and the freedom

---

1 The artwork and accompanying descriptions throughout this commentary were prepared by Hannah Lewis.

1

that brings. This is in contrast to other deaf people in the painting who are restricted by the limits of having to try and communicate only by speaking and lip-reading. The smile on the signing figure, as well as its being painted in a different colour, shows the joy of being free to communicate in their own language. Similarly, the aliens and exiles of 1 Peter are being encouraged to find joy and freedom in their identity in Christ. When we become aware that, because of our faith, we are the odd one out in our own cultural context, do we beam with this freedom?

Nancy Rourke, deaf artist, used by permission; the coloured version can be accessed at www.nancyrourke.com/paintings/deaf/lifeisshort.jpg.

The first chapter of 1 Peter sets the tone for the whole of the letter. From the first verse we are told that the letter is from 'Peter, an apostle of Jesus Christ' (1.1) and is written to 'exiles' who are spread throughout Asia Minor. The identity of these dispersed exiles is not limited to their geographical situation and dislocation, but immediately they are identified as 'chosen', 'destined' and 'sanctified' by Jesus Christ (1.2). This identity is crucial to the whole of the letter and for the apostolic author's understanding of God, for God the Father has chosen these exiles as God's own, the Spirit has made these exiles holy and they are called to obey Jesus Christ.

The first chapter builds on this new identity in

Jesus Christ through six themes that run across the letter. **Diaspora and living as resident aliens** is the first theme for these are the ones who make up the community of 1 Peter. They are called 'strangers in the world', exiles or resident aliens (1.1, 17) who are experiencing or have experienced persecution. This context will form the basis for the call not only to hope, holiness and joy, but also to hospitality, risk, witness, resistance and resilience. **Hope** is the second theme, whose foundation is Jesus Christ. Hope in Christ is not the same as optimism, for only hope can confront death and despair because this hope is based on the death and resurrection of Christ and not on our own doings or personal piety. This leads straight into the third theme, that of **rebirth and resurrection.** The movement from death to life (1.3) is connected to the resurrection of Jesus Christ (1.19–20) and to the calling as God's own people (1.22–23). This rebirth through the living word of God moves one from no hope to hope (1.21), from ignorance to knowledge (1.14), from disobedience to obedience (1.2, 22).

Peter's letter is addressed to those who are suffering. Difficult as it may sound, the apostolic call is to rejoice in the midst of suffering and testing (1.6) and to know **Christ's joy in the midst of suffering.** With the focus on Christ, those who are suffering now are assured of the work of God to bring new life in which the past is forgiven, the present protected and the future assured (1.3–5, 7). The joy of Christ is thus shared even when he is not seen (1.8), and his suffering and glory is the example and encouragement to these dispersed Christians (1.11).

Christ's self-sacrifice and suffering also informs the fifth theme, which is the **call to holiness** of those who bear the name 'Christian'. This is a call to imitate God in God's self-sacrificial movement towards the other and towards us. God is holy and so we too are called to be holy (1.15–16). This holiness is not something that we can earn or control, but is an invitation and a gift, which leads to the final theme of 1 Peter: **inheritance and God's gift**. God's gifts are better than gold or silver (1.18) and can never perish, spoil, or fade (1.4). And while holiness, hope and being chosen as God's own people are all gifts from God, the ultimate gift described within 1 Peter is that of salvation (1.5, 9, 10).

---

1 Peter 1.1–2

[1] Peter, an apostle of Jesus Christ, to the exiles of the Dispersion in Pontus, Galatia, Cappadocia, Asia, and Bithynia, [2] who have been chosen and destined by God the Father and sanctified by the Spirit to be obedient to Jesus Christ and to be sprinkled with his blood:

May grace and peace be yours in abundance.

---

1 Peter is a general letter sent to Christians dispersed in the Roman provinces or regions of Asia Minor. These are places in the Roman Empire that are known for their faith, but many of them are places to which Paul did not travel in his missionary journeys (see Acts 16.7). The very first word of the letter makes clear that it is attributed to the apostle Peter. As suggested in the earlier introduction, scholars debate whether Peter could have written it directly because of its sophisticated Greek syntax. The letter's contents also suggest that it was written towards the end of the first century (Bartlett, p. 234). Thus, some advocate that it was written after Peter's death perhaps by a ghostwriter such as Mark or Silvanus (mentioned in 1 Peter 5). Whether the letter was written by Peter or some other early Christian leader, the letter is deliberately cast in the character of Peter and written by an author who lived in diaspora in the imperial centre of Rome to colonial subjects living in Asia Minor.

Asia Minor had been colonized for centuries and was influenced by Hellenistic language and culture, as well as Roman imperial commerce and religion (Schüssler Fiorenza, p. 383). The recipients of the letter are characterized as exiles, migrants, foreigners and resident aliens (1.1; 2.11). It is worth noting, in this Roman context, that there are two meanings of the word 'exile' in the opening of the letter. First, in its immediate context, 'exile' means that the Christians who received the letter had left their homeland to live as strangers and foreigners in Asia Minor. In this sense, the word establishes a connection between the sender and the recipients as they are both living in exile, in diaspora. Second, 'exile' may also mean that all Christians no matter their political or geographical context are living in exile, separated for a time from their eternal home in heaven (Bartlett, p. 246).

The language of 'exile' and 'dispersion' or diaspora in the opening sentence of 1 Peter is key as it draws on well-known images and experiences from the Old Testament, where Israel was scattered like sheep as resident aliens in a foreign land. This is also an image picked up later in 1 Peter 2 and 5, where Peter draws on Ezekiel 34 and Gospel stories such as Luke 15, with God and Christ as a shepherd looking for scattered, lost sheep.

Those who are exiles, separated from their home, are outsiders and often reviled. Resident aliens did not have full citizenship and did not enjoy the protection and rights that they once did in their homeland. They were politically and economically exploited and vulnerable, and often had to endure disdain and suspicion by those who were citizens. They could not hold major civic offices and were restricted in commerce, intermarriage and land tenure. However, they were still responsible for taxes and military services. Their status was not very different from foreigners and migrants (Elliott 1990, p. 26; Schüssler Fiorenza, p. 386). Their condition could be compared to Jewish exiles who did not live in their homeland and were treated as second-class citizens.

Therefore, from the beginning we see that the recipients of 1 Peter suffered from rejection and harassment by members of society because they lived as strangers in a foreign land and their Christian identity made them suspect. They were once pagans, following the religious and social practices of their ancestors (1.18), but they have become Christians, chosen by God and sanctified by the Holy Spirit (1.2). And this is the focus of the consolation and encouragement to the recipients of this letter. In the world, their sharing in the name of Christ may lead to suffering, but they are chosen, destined, belonging to a new people and protected by the power of God (1.3–5).

The letter exhorts Christians living in diaspora to put their faith in God and not lose hope in an environment of suspicion and hostility. As minorities in a colonized world, they had to show how living as a Christian community was different while, at the same time, they needed to bear witness that their Christian way of living did not present a threat to society. One of the challenges of 1 Peter is how it expresses truth and encouragement to those who are persecuted and who live in danger because of their faith. It is difficult for those who are not persecuted to understand the reality of the recipients of this letter and there is much potential for disconnect and judgement.

1 Peter is highly relevant today, as the twenty-first century has been called 'the century of migration'. The letter touches on the themes of exile, diaspora, migration, interreligious relationships, living as minorities, second-class citizenship, gender relations and relationships to authorities. The strategies the letter offers to the suffering Christians in Asia Minor may not be applicable to all Christians living in different parts of the world today. Yet, it offers a mirror for us to examine power dynamics both in the public and domestic sphere.

Excursus: Home and Homelessness

1 Peter is addressed to Gentile converts who find themselves rootless because of their new affiliation. They are now 'exiles of the Dispersion' (1.1) and 'aliens' (2.11). Discontented or no longer welcome in their original homes, they have become homeless. Yet the letter balances titles of dispossession and instability with images of possession and stability. Believers are now living stones in a new building, a 'spiritual house' (2.5). They now share the inheritance of God's people Israel ('a chosen race, a royal priesthood, a holy nation', 2.9; see also Ex. 19.6). Those who appeared to be without a home now find a common home in the 'house' or 'household of God' (4.17).

1 Peter 1.3–5

[3] Blessed be the God and Father of our Lord Jesus Christ! By his great mercy he has given us a new birth into a living hope through the resurrection of Jesus Christ from the dead, [4] and into an inheritance that is imperishable, undefiled, and unfading, kept in heaven for you, [5] who are being protected by the power of God through faith for a salvation ready to be revealed in the last time.

As the opening to 1 Peter continues, hope remains central not as something that we deserve, but as something that we are given. The letter describes two gifts, given through God's great mercy: a 'new birth' into 'living hope' ('living' is an adjective Peter is especially fond of) and a heavenly inheritance. The first gift of 'living hope' is grounded in the resurrection of Jesus Christ. The second gift is a heavenly inheritance which is described as 'imperishable, undefiled, and unfading' (1.4). This heavenly inheritance is connected to the promise of salvation, already achieved by Christ and 'ready to be revealed'.

Hope cannot be separated from the life that Jesus offers in his death and resurrection. It is not based on wishful thinking, fantasy, hyperbole, or any propaganda promoted by the empire or those pretending to have God's authority. Neither does such hope ever reduce to mere optimism, as if it were like a secular 'hope' for good weather or the success of one's football team. It is instead secure and anchored in God. This is the biblical mark of hope; it is always characterized by God's assured redemptive future already reaching out towards us, yet never in our grasp by skill or power (see Bockmuehl 2012a).

Faithful hope, living hope, is thus refined and strengthened, rather than subverted, by the experience of trials and suffering. Such refinement and testing of hope is sustained through the believers' love for Jesus Christ, being filled with 'indescribable and glorious joy' at the assured outcome of faith in the salvation 'ready to be revealed'. And this assured outcome of faith in salvation is the promise found in 1 Peter 1.4 of the inheritance 'kept in heaven for you'. The word 'kept' makes clear this is not something an individual can do or achieve but that God is the one who reserves the inheritance for believers. Peter emphasizes the security and certainty of the reward awaiting his community.

The promise of 'new birth' in 1.3 means being part of a new family and therefore a new citizenship that bestows greater benefits than anything Rome or any power doing its bidding can offer. It also means victory over any power that opposes God. Because of rebirth through the resurrection of Jesus Christ, the community of 1 Peter is offered the possibility of new beginnings, new possibilities and transformation for them not just as individuals but as communities of people who follow Jesus Christ. The message of hope to all is that we are not bound by our present circumstances, challenges and troubles.

There is, therefore, a glorious promise in 1 Peter 1.5 for those who call themselves 'Christian'. God's power may not shield believers from trials and sufferings, but it does protect them from that which would cause them to fall away. God's power protects because God's power is the means by which faith is sustained. The ultimate reason for preservation must be God's gift rather than any individual act of faith since otherwise the reference to God's power is unnecessary. Its function is to encourage believers with the truth that God will preserve their faith through sufferings and the changes of life. Faith and hope are ultimately gifts of God, and Peter is clear that God promises to fortify believers – to protect those whose hope is in God – so that they persist in faith and hope until the day that they obtain the promised inheritance.

1 Peter 1.6–12

[6] In this you rejoice, even if now for a little while you have had to suffer various trials, [7] so that the genuineness of your faith – being more precious than gold that, though perishable, is tested by fire – may be found to result in praise and glory and honour when Jesus Christ is revealed. [8] Although you have not seen him, you love him; and even though you do not see him now, you believe in him and rejoice with an indescribable and glorious joy, [9] for you are receiving the outcome of your faith, the salvation of your souls.

[10] Concerning this salvation, the prophets who prophesied of the grace that was to be yours made careful search and inquiry, [11] inquiring about the person or time that the Spirit of Christ within them indicated, when it testified in advance to the sufferings destined for Christ and the subsequent glory. [12] It was revealed to them that they were serving not themselves but you, in regard to the things that have now been announced to you through those who brought you good news by the Holy Spirit sent from heaven – things into which angels long to look!

The letter continues to build on the connection between hope, inheritance, salvation and Christ, whom the readers may not have seen, but they nevertheless love him, believe in him and rejoice with him. Christian hope is closely patterned on the experience of Jesus himself: his suffering and death (1.19; 2.21), but equally his resurrection (1.21) and exaltation (3.21). This logic of a union with Christ in hope and holy discipleship defines and structures our new birth and new behaviour (Achtemeier, p. 66). New birth to living hope in Christ alters our 'patriotic' allegiances as well: formerly enfranchised and at home in the world (1.14; 4.4), our true home in God now makes us exiled and alienated from secular society's social, moral and spiritual loyalties (1.1, 17; 2.11). Such alienation is at times necessarily uncomfortable: its witness entails suffering, opposition and rejection by contemporaries who prize these loyalties we have left behind – again compared to the witness of Jesus (1.6; 2.18–20; 3.14, 17; 4.12; see Elliott 2000, p. 314).

The significant words in this section of the letter, which some may be surprised to find together, are 'joy', 'good news' and 'suffering'. The word for 'good news' is the same as that for 'gospel' and occurs twice in this chapter, once in this section and once at the end. Peter ensures his community knows that all of his letter is good news 'announced to you' (1.25). Moreover, Peter offers what he sees as a summary of the gospel, which leads to nothing less than the 'salvation of your souls' (1.9). This promise of salvation is connected by Peter to the salvation history of all God's people, beginning with the prophets who also 'testified in advance' to the promise of salvation and 'prophesied of the grace that was to be made yours' (1.11, 10). Similar to the Gospels in some ways, Peter seeks to find fulfilment of all of the scriptures, including the prophets, in Christ (see Keener 2013).

This proclamation of God's promise of salvation is immediately linked by Peter to essential elements of faith, namely joy, love and believing. Peter teaches, in line with many other teachers in Scripture, that faith is not something necessarily seen, but is deeply connected to love and joy. And both love and joy remind the reader that even while they have to 'suffer various trials' they are part of something greater than they can see and such suffering is not eternal ('for a little while'; 1.6). By connecting his community both to the prophets and the way God has acted in the past, and to the future and the promises of heaven (1.12), Peter seeks to comfort and to empower those who are suffering. Peter calls those who are suffering to faith, hope and joy, even as at times they struggle to survive.

Hope and joy, therefore, are deeply connected to the reality that those who follow Christ and suffer for Christ are part of something larger, which goes beyond the immediate. And thus, in a sense, Christian mission is not simply about individual joy and individual hope, but the witness of joy and hope in the midst of struggle, suffering and even persecution. We remember that this letter is written to those who are living scattered in the world as a minority in their culture. In this context, the good news is proclaimed, raising the question for Christians both then and now about what the Spirit is doing in the Church, scattered around the world and in some places hidden, fearful and oppressed. How is Christ revealed in such contexts? Peter exhorts his community to embrace joy in the midst of suffering and rejection. Peter makes clear that this exhortation is good news and that this gospel, revealed in Jesus Christ, is what binds them together as a resurrection people called to new birth.

This promise of hope and new birth, then, is no mere religious mood music to make us feel comfortable and 'affirmed'. The gifts of new life patterned on the witness of Jesus are indeed both openly inclusive, welcoming *everyone* as they are – and yet radically transformative, leaving no one 'just the way I am'. Hope in Christ transforms both our fears and our desires, freeing us from our sinful and self-destructive past allegiances, as we see in the next section of the letter (1.14, 18–19). Hope and holiness are linked in an inalienable embrace: to set one's hope on Christ is in every aspect of life to become holy as he is holy, which also continually entails sobering up to 'prepare your minds for action' (1.13, 15–16).

> ## 1 Peter 1.13–16
>
> [13] Therefore prepare your minds for action; discipline yourselves; set all your hope on the grace that Jesus Christ will bring you when he is revealed. [14] Like obedient children, do not be conformed to the desires that you formerly had in ignorance. [15] Instead, as he who called you is holy, be holy yourselves in all your conduct; [16] for it is written, 'You shall be holy, for I am holy.'

In many ways, this section (1.13–16) functions as the centrepiece of the entire chapter. Compare the manner by which these verses are introduced by the word 'Therefore …'. In this section, Peter moves to a call to action, to discipline, to hope and to holiness. The call to holiness is especially significant, as it is a theme that runs through the whole of the letter. Within this chapter, explicit references can be found in 1.2 ('sanctified/made holy by the Spirit') and 1.14–16 ('he who has called you is holy, be holy yourselves'). Clear allusions to the same theme are also found in 1.4 with the 'undefiled' nature of the inheritance kept in heaven; 1.7 speaking about the significance of testing by fire; and the description of Christ in 1.19 as 'a lamb without defect or blemish'. The call to holiness represents an invitation into the life of the triune God; it reveals that which has been made gloriously possible in the good news. As such, holiness is presented both as a condition or state granted to believers through Christ (1.4, 14–16, 19) and as a goal or outcome to which they themselves must attain (1.2, 7, 22). The vocation, the call, of all is to holiness and to God.

The 'given-ness' of holiness is essentially the reality of who Christ is, and forever will be, for all who come to trust in him. It serves as a reminder to believers of their new-found status before God.[2] They are made holy by him, and this in turn links contextually with the themes elsewhere in this chapter of 'new birth', 'hope' and 'gift'. Further, this establishment of believers' holy standing before God cannot be undone. It is unchanging, unconditional, already perfect and fully guaranteed. Conversely, the sense whereby believers are expected to conform to a new standard of moral holiness serves as an inescapable call to transformed living. This aspect of incremental holiness focuses on the believers' walk, and in 1 Peter this can be interpreted both individually and in terms of communal identity.

In contrast to the security and constancy of their holy status, the requirement to demonstrate holy living through walking with Christ is liable to fluctuation, to circumstances, to personal choices and to intermittent progress. In this regard, therefore, the experiential nature of holiness can be connected

2 The distinction between 'status' and 'walk' for believers is helpfully unpacked by Matt Fuller.

to the themes of maintaining joy in face of hard-ship and suffering and of what it means to live as 'resident aliens'. Many and relentless pressures, both external and internal, will be brought to bear against the believers' desire to live holy lives. These may be arduous, but ultimately their impact can be purposeful, if understood through the filter of precisely what the chapter and the letter are aiming to teach: Pursue such holiness because the one who calls you is holy (1.15). In regard to all of this, there is a pressing need for the exercise of personal responsibility, and this expression of human effort in no way prevents the grace and operation of the Spirit, but rather, and somewhat counterintuitively, manifests and facilitates it.

Thus, as we can see, 1 Peter is saturated with a concern for holiness and discusses this holiness in more than an abstract or even in a purely behavioural way. While the concept of holiness is often associated with 'separation' or distinction – God's distinction from what is unholy – this truth can give the false impression that holiness is about distance and exclusion. A more accurate view of holiness in biblical terms would see it as the character of God's movement to embrace and transform what is far from God, a movement which, especially in the light of sin, 'costs' God something. Holiness is therefore not an abstention from the bad, but an imitation of God in God's self-sacrificial movement towards the other, which is most explicit in the person of Jesus Christ. As such, holiness is not about exclusion but the transformation of all that is not holy into something that is good. In this way, imitating God's movement towards us should determine the action, the discipline, the behaviour (we could say, the ethics) within the Christian community and communion. God seeks a creation that reflects divine truth, beauty and goodness; holiness is how God achieves this.

Here we see that holiness isn't about performative piety, nor is it something that a Christian can earn. Rather it is given by God, it is a call from God and it leads to transformation. As such, one does not have to have certain abilities to be holy: the marginalized, the weak, the disabled can all be holy. In the Old Testament, from which 1 Peter draws numerous images, holiness is something that is discussed in terms of the history of God's relationship with Israel. So in 1 Peter, holiness is treated as a characteristic of a great divine movement, embodied in Jesus Christ. The Son of God comes into the world, lives a certain kind of life, and in doing so takes to himself a people. This people, in turn, is carried along in a life lived within the world that is joined to the life of Christ. It is important to see holiness in terms of this divine movement. For, given in Christ, this movement is offered to human beings as the very shape of Christian identity.

The quotation of Leviticus 19.2 that we find in 1.16 – 'You shall be holy, for I am holy' – deliberately and emphatically grounds holiness in the revealed nature of God and the Old Testament. Within the narrative of the exodus wanderings, for example, God's holiness is intended to become a pattern for God's people to imitate. In this there is a further echoing of the 'walk' motif, the idea of journeying spiritually with, and deeper into, God, even as God's people find themselves surrounded by an alien and potentially oppressive culture. The injunction of holiness is double-edged, alluding to a life of separation and devotion on the one hand and to a spirit of perseverance and resilience on the other.

When we look at this theme across 1 Peter, we see that the call to a holy life in 1.15–16 finds its embodiment in being a 'holy priesthood' in 2.5, offering spiritual sacrifices. And this in turn is elaborated in 2.9 in terms of the life of a 'holy people'. All of this – holy life, holy sacrifice, holy peoplehood – is then explained in terms of a single and marvellous act by God, outlined in 2.10: God calls us out of darkness into light, turning nobodies into a nation, bestowing divine forgiveness on the unforgiven. The entire act of God described here constitutes the life, passion, death and resurrection of Jesus, the self-giving of God for sinful human beings, that takes them with him to his own glory. Holiness, then, is supremely manifest in God *coming close* to the *un*holy, patiently submitting to what is unholy, and thereby transforming it to God's own character of self-sacrificing love. This is a central

Gospel proclamation: 'But God proves his love for us in that while we still were sinners Christ died for us' (Rom. 5.8). This proclamation is then given a form within human life and relationship: 'Love your enemies' (Matt. 5.44; Luke 6.27, 35).

Holiness in 1 Peter, therefore, has a profound centre in Christ since it describes the act of God in Christ moving towards what is unholy in order to transform it: what were but 'stones' become 'living' (2.5); those who were 'not a people' become 'God's people' (2.10); those who are 'scattered', 'strangers' and 'lost' (1.1; 2.11, 25), are gathered together 'in Christ' (5.14; 2.25). This body of Christ (see Eph. 2.16), which is given over in suffering for others (2.24), becomes the shared 'calling' of the Church (2.12).

Holiness, then, involves distinction and behaviour, but primarily as aspects of sacrifice, where what is true, good and beautiful is offered up for the sake of others in love. As Christians are joined to Christ, they share in Christ's divine character; and as they love with Christ, they display and receive his divine treasure. The Church's holiness, then, is one oriented to others: not only to the holy within the Church, but to the unholy within and outside the Church. Jesus is the only one who can make the unholy holy. We might separate ourselves because we have judged another to be unholy. And yet, the call of the Christian is to live on the border of the holy just as Jesus himself loved and broke bread

with those considered 'unholy' in his own time.
Christ even became sin for us, dying an unholy
death as a criminal on a cross, in order to draw
the whole world to himself. The call to holiness is
always derivative, grounded in Christ. A person
is holy, the Church is holy, a community is holy,
only because Christ is in the midst of it. Holiness
is therefore a movement of sacrifice and of love
which is embraced so that the world might in fact
be changed and reflect the glory which is 'revealed'
finally in the fullness of God's movement of love for
the world in Christ (4.13, 14; 5.4, 10).

1 Peter 1.17–25

[17] If you invoke as Father the one who judges all people
impartially according to their deeds, live in reverent
fear during the time of your exile. [18] You know that
you were ransomed from the futile ways inherited
from your ancestors, not with perishable things like
silver or gold, [19] but with the precious blood of Christ,
like that of a lamb without defect or blemish. [20] He
was destined before the foundation of the world, but
was revealed at the end of the ages for your sake.
[21] Through him you have come to trust in God, who
raised him from the dead and gave him glory, so that
your faith and hope are set on God. [22] Now that you
have purified your souls by your obedience to the

> truth so that you have genuine mutual love, love one
> another deeply from the heart. [23] You have been born
> anew, not of perishable but of imperishable seed,
> through the living and enduring word of God. [24] For
>
> 'All flesh is like grass
>   and all its glory like the flower of grass.
> The grass withers,
>   and the flower falls,
> [25] but the word of the Lord endures for ever.'
> That word is the good news that was announced to
> you.

Peter uses the language of 'inheritance' to describe
what is in store for Christians. In the Old Testament, inheritance is the land God promised to God's
people (Num. 32.19; Deut. 2.12; 12.9; 25.19; 26.1;
Josh. 11.23; Ps. 105.11; also Acts 7.5). Peter understands inheritance, however, no longer in terms of a
land promised to Israel but in terms of the end-time
hope that lies before believers. The recipients of this
letter are sojourners and aliens in this world, they
are exiles who face suffering now and their hope is
directed to the future inheritance.

Peter gives to inheritance a content that is beyond
human history – an inheritance that is imperishable,
undefiled, and unfading, kept in heaven for you
(1.4). The crucial means to this living hope is the

resurrection of Jesus Christ from the dead (1.3, 21). Thus, the event of Jesus' resurrection makes the hope of future resurrection a present reality and becomes the basis for the future imperishable inheritance.

The language of imperishability is found throughout this first chapter, and especially in this final section. The significance of this term is that the promised inheritance, given 'with the precious blood of Christ', can never perish or be corrupted. Elsewhere in the New Testament we are told that God is imperishable (Rom. 1.23; 1 Tim. 1.17) and that our resurrection bodies are incorruptible (1 Cor. 15.22). Within the Old Testament and in the context of God's work throughout history, the land of Israel was at times ravaged and destroyed by invading armies. The prophet Isaiah describes the utter destruction of the whole world in God's judgement: The earth will be completely laid waste and totally plundered (Isa. 24.3). In the Greek version of Isaiah, the word for 'laid waste' and 'wither' is the same that Peter uses. But Peter uses the word in a negative form. The world will be destroyed, but our inheritance is indestructible, it is imperishable.

The inheritance, however, is not only imperishable but it is also without blemish, it cannot spoil, it is 'undefiled'. The inheritance will not lose its lustre and beauty. It will never become stained or filthy. The same word is used to denote Jesus' sinlessness

(Heb. 7.26), the purity of marriage (Heb. 13.4) and genuine religion (James 1.27). Isaiah, just quoted, goes on to tell how people have defiled the earth by breaking God's law. In the prophecy of Jeremiah, too, God declares that he gave Israel a fertile land, but 'you defiled my land, and made my heritage an abomination' (Jer. 2.7). In contrast, the inheritance Peter speaks about is undefiled and undefilable.

This inheritance, like the word of God, also endures for ever (1.24), it will never 'fade'. It will last forever, just as the crown of reward that elders receive will never fade away (5.4). Our inheritance is lasting, God's action in Christ is eternal. It will not fade, wither or dry up like grass. Isaiah reflects on the judgements of God that cause the land and its inhabitants to wither like grass or flowers: 'The grass withers and the flowers fall, but the word of our God stands for ever' (Isa. 40.8). Peter quotes that passage at the end of this chapter, and again uses the word we read as 'imperishable' (1.23). Because the inheritance described by Peter is in heaven, nothing on earth can alter or destroy it. Peter must use negative terms to describe it ('imperishable', 'undefiled', 'unfading'; 1.4) because its reality surpasses our present comprehension.

The chapter concludes with themes that have run throughout, reminding readers that everything – fear, promise, faith, hope, love, rebirth – is connected to Jesus Christ. The language of being 'born anew' through the 'living and enduring word of

God' remains a central promise of this letter. For just as hope is not stagnant but is living, so too God's word is not stagnant in this world. And this word promises that the God who raised Jesus from the dead and gave him glory (1.21), will also welcome all those who 'trust in God' into the joy of future glory, 'revealed at the end of the ages for your sake' (1.20).

While Peter might end this chapter with the reminder that this salvation will not be unveiled until the last day – it is a future event – he does not leave them without hope in their time of exile. For Peter calls the community to mutual love and to unity in Christ in his death and resurrection in a way that supersedes all despair, all division and all that is perishable in this world. The call to 'love one another deeply from the heart' is the focus at the end of this first chapter, and is the response that the saving act of God in Christ demands. The resurrection, therefore, is an essential part of the living hope to which Peter calls his community and it is what enables the Christian to stand firm against all that brings death in individual lives, in communities, in this world. The resurrection gives hope and courage to rise up against all that seeks to kill, enabling hope, instilling love and grounding confidence, even in the midst of suffering, in the word of God which endures for ever (1.25).

Excursus: Aliens and Exiles

As we move into the second chapter, Peter continues to address his community as 'aliens and exiles' and urges them to abstain from the passions of the flesh (2.11). The terms 'aliens' and 'exiles' are two different words in Greek. The word for 'alien' derives from a Hebrew word that has many translations, such as 'sojourner', 'foreigner', 'stranger', 'immigrant', and 'resident alien'. The biblical term also refers to a non-Israelite who has no familial or tribal affiliation with those Israelites among whom she or he is living. Therefore, he or she is not treated as a permanent resident and frequently does not have full rights within the community (a situation that we may find in many twenty-first-century societies). Similarly, the term for 'exile' has been translated as 'stranger' or 'foreigner'. There is no consensus as to how best to translate these two terms, but there is agreement that they refer to different ways of being a stranger or outsider; basically they refer to someone who has taken temporary abode in a land that is not his or hers. The Israelites were reminded to show compassion and care to aliens and strangers since they were once 'strangers' in a foreign land, namely Egypt (see Lev. 19.34).

1 Peter reminds the believers that they are 'aliens and exiles' because of their allegiance to Jesus Christ. They are exhorted not to conform to the social and religious norms of society, thereby demonstrating their distinctiveness. Peter also encourages them to engage with the society so as to dispel any suspicions people might have about believers, and furthermore to gain their praise. In other words, Peter emphasizes that the conduct of the believers should be rooted in identity in Christ and as 'aliens and exiles'.

Questions for reflection

1 1 Peter is written to a people described as 'resident aliens' who live as exiles and strangers in the world.

- Who are the exiles, strangers, or aliens in your part of the world?
- How does your faith in Christ make you an alien or stranger in your world?
- How does such an identity help you to minister to those who are exiles and strangers in your community?

2 1 Peter calls his community to embody a 'living hope'.
   • What does hope look like in your life?
   • When has hope in Christ helped you in your life?

3 1 Peter speaks in depth about holiness, calling believers to be holy as God is holy.
   • How does it change your understanding of holiness if you see it as a gift and not something you can earn?
   • What does living a holy life look like?

2

A Holy People
Following Christ
(1 Peter 2)

Herodian cornerstones in Jerusalem.

Herodian cornerstones: Peter writes, 'See, I am laying in Zion a stone, a cornerstone chosen and precious' (2.6). This photo is of a cornerstone of the temple mount in Jerusalem – part of the temple that survived the destruction by the Romans in 70 CE and 2,000 years of turbulent history since. The large stones pictured are up to 12m x 2.4m x 1m in size. They weigh about 80 tons each. The sheer size and weight of these stones helps stabilize the structure and each stone is carefully chosen so there are no faults and cracks that would build a weakness into the wall. If we look at these stones, we can reflect that this is the foundation on which our faith is built – Jesus our cornerstone – and if we rest on him, we can depend on his strength.

Herodian cornerstones in Jerusalem, image courtesy of J. Straw-bridge.

The opening of 1 Peter 2 continues the momentum of chapter 1, beginning with a warning to avoid malice and guile and all that might undermine the unity of the community and the mutual love they are to show one another. Abandoning malice and false-hood is the consequence of loving one another and having been born anew in Christ. One key element of the ethics of 1 Peter, therefore, is not holding hatred, guile, insincerity or envy towards those with whom we disagree. From the start, 1 Peter 2 is focused on the identity of the community in Christ. If God's word – the good news that was announced to believers (1.25) – is like milk that helps infants to grow, then believers should be hungry for it (2.2). Indeed, it is the Lord himself who nourishes believers with his goodness (2.3; see Ps. 34.8).

The bulk of chapter 2 is taken up with the metaphor of the 'living stone'. Jesus is described with that title (2.4), and those who believe in Jesus are as well (2.5). The language of 'living' applies not only to hope and to God's word as in 1 Peter 1, but also to God's people and to Christ. The imagery of the stone comes from the Old Testament. It is found in Isaiah (8.14; 28.16) and in the Psalms (118.22). As elsewhere in the New Testament, the author here draws on the Old Testament and interprets it in light of the Church's experience of faith in Jesus. Jesus and believers together live into, or 'fulfil', the words and imagery found in the Old Testament. Believers in Jesus inherit the calling that God gave to Israel to be 'a chosen race, a royal priesthood, a holy nation, God's own people' (1 Peter 2.9, drawing on Ex. 19.6 and Isa. 43.20–21).

Israel was chosen by God to be 'a light to the nations' (Isa. 49.6). Likewise, says Peter, believers in Jesus are to 'proclaim the mighty acts of [God] who called you out of darkness into his marvellous light' (2.9). Even in the face of hostility and persecution, 1 Peter insists believers should strive to live in such a way that the Gentiles among whom they reside may 'see your honourable deeds and glorify God when he comes to judge' (2.12). Peter recognizes this will not be easy. Sometimes living peaceably will involve enduring harsh treatment (2.18) and bearing up under unjust discipline (2.19). Peter offers teachings at the end of chapter 2 and into chapter 3 of how to be a Christian in three very specific situations in the world: how Christians are to live in relation to the state, how Christian slaves are to live in relation to masters and how Christian wives and husbands are to live in relationship with one another. Through it all, 1 Peter promises that Christ's saving work and righteous example will provide the motivation and the strength that believers need in order to persevere (2.21–25).

One of the challenges in interpreting 1 Peter is deciding how the letter constructs its theological argument. On this front, unfortunately, the chapter divisions of the letter are not terribly helpful. As we will expand in this chapter and the next, 2.13–25 is inseparable from 3.1–7, where the letter calls various sectors of the Church to 'accept the authority of' (2.13, 18; 3.1). An understanding of the letter's argument requires locating the three summonses to 'accept the authority of' within an argument that includes at least 1 Peter 2.11–3.7, but also 3.8–17 as the next chapter will make clear. In other words, 1 Peter 2 cannot be disconnected from 1 Peter 3 and, in fact, does not make sense without reading the letter through the chapter break.

A close examination of 1 Peter 2 suggests that the second chapter as a whole can be divided into clear sections where Peter encourages his listeners to 'grow into salvation' (2.1–3) and clearly delineates the Christian identity as the elect and holy people of God (2.4–10). Having articulated the importance of Christian growth and the characteristics of the 'elect', Peter describes aspects of Christian conduct that should follow in relation to key social structures (2.11–3.12).

Excursus: Perspectives and Power in 1 Peter 2

The first letter of Peter is addressed to 'aliens and exiles' (2.11), a theme already encountered in chapter 1. It is possible to read this phrase as referring to a people who are strangers; landless and powerless within the structures of the society in which they find themselves. Certainly we know that the Christ-followers of Peter's community included slaves and perhaps others in a similar lowly position in society. So, if we read chapter 2 from the perspective of the landless and the powerless, what does it say to them and to us?

This letter has been read (and preached) as teaching such people simply to accept their lot in life and to submit to authority; but it is possible to read this chapter in a much more subversive (and therefore constructive) light. If we assume that, like slaves, 'aliens and exiles' are not in a position to change their social situation, we can ask how they might cope with and live in such circumstances. They may not be able to make a material change to their situation, but do they have an option relating to how they see themselves and their humanity? Have they internalized their situation, perceiving themselves as lesser humans? Or, with the encouragement of 1 Peter, might they be able to claim their dignity as children of God, despite being powerless in other ways? The text of 2.16 exhorts them to 'live as free people' – perhaps not externally free but liberated in the way they see themselves.

To such people – then as well as now – the promises of 1 Peter 2 are of no small significance. A people told that once they were 'not a people' – they were ignored, marginalized, demeaned, shamed – are told that they are 'now God's people' (2.10). A people told they are shameful, exiled and on the margins of their society are in fact 'God's own people' (2.9). They are holy as God is holy, they are 'a chosen race and a royal priesthood' (2.9), they are 'chosen and precious in God's sight' (2.4). These people are told that, although they are lost and confused, Christ the cornerstone will give them direction (2.6). These people are told that their identity as 'stranger', 'exile' and 'odd one out' has been transformed. Previously this identity as a stranger was a mark of shame but now it is a sign that they are God's own people. Those who are slaves are told they are in fact free – free to choose to obey, internally sure of their dignity; resilient and resistant – because they know that the one who walks by their side through the suffering is Christ himself (2.21).

These messages find their utmost expression in the passage about living stones (2.4–8). In a society where power and status were shown through the construction of great monuments or of temples with elaborate carved columns, these powerless and landless (and possibly poor) people were not able to 'compete' with their more affluent neighbours in the pursuit of honour. They were likewise not able to demonstrate their faith in God's power through building large and elaborate places of worship. Peter's first letter, however, challenges prevailing ideas about power and status, saying that believers are *living* stones and that they build *living* temples with their own bodies (2.5) – their own despised, neglected, poor and perhaps beaten bodies – to witness to Christ their cornerstone in that way. They witness to the Christ who himself was despised and neglected but who transformed that through his resurrection.

This challenge to and transformation of the way the world understands power and status in chapter 2 begins with tasting the pure spiritual milk of Christ, the Word of God (2.2) and ends in returning to Christ the shepherd and guardian of their souls (2.25).

1 Peter 2.1–3

[1] Rid yourselves, therefore, of all malice, and all guile, insincerity, envy, and all slander. [2] Like newborn infants, long for the pure spiritual milk, so that by it you may grow into salvation – [3] if indeed you have tasted that the Lord is good.

In this opening section, Peter exhorts his listeners to 'lay aside' or rid themselves of vices that are harmful to the community. Similar 'vice-catalogues' can be found in some of Paul's letters (1 Cor. 5.10–11; Gal. 5.19–21; Eph. 5.3–5; Col. 3.5, 8). The vices stated in Peter's list are attitudes and behaviours that could destroy the community: malice, deceit, insincerity, envy and slander. Therefore, the community is encouraged to behave righteously towards one another. Furthermore, just like 'newborn infants', Peter's recipients are to 'long for' or 'crave' the 'pure spiritual milk' that would give them life. One might get the impression that Peter is addressing new converts because of terms such as 'newborn infants' and 'milk' but he is not. He is, on the contrary, addressing a community who understand themselves as 'born-again' Christians in the face of a hostile society and who are in need of 'spiritual milk' for their continued spiritual growth.

The 'spiritual milk' Peter speaks of must refer to the word of God that brings new life into being and which will continue to nourish the lives of Peter's readers and listeners (see also 1.23, 25; 2.8). This nourishment comes to them through Scripture, the teaching and preaching of the Church and bearing witness to the mighty acts of God (2.9). For Peter, the divine 'milk' of the word of God is 'something Christians must never outgrow' (Boring, p. 93).

The verse that serves to link the present section to what follows is 1 Peter 2.3, which utilizes a word play between 'tasted' and 'spiritual milk'. Having been nourished by the 'spiritual milk', the community can vouch that the Lord is good. On that basis, in the next section, Peter urges his audience to draw near to Christ who is the 'living stone, though rejected by mortals yet chosen and precious to God's sight' (2.4). Thereby, Peter begins to define his listeners' Christian identity as an elect and holy people.

Excursus: Characterizations of Jesus in 1 Peter 2

What can we learn about the character and actions of Jesus Christ in 1 Peter 2? In this chapter, there are at least four themes that can lead us into a deeper understanding of who Jesus is for us today.

First, 1 Peter 2 portrays Jesus as a 'living stone' (2.4). Stones that are 'living' are those that haven't

yet been quarried – that are still 'alive' and grow-
ing through sedimentation. Paradoxically, though,
1 Peter says that Christ has already been fitted by
God to be 'a cornerstone chosen and precious ...,
the very head of the corner' (2.6, 7). God the
stonemason has selected Jesus to be the key part
of the foundation of 'a spiritual house' (2.5). Jesus
can fulfil this role because, although he died by
crucifixion, he is now 'living' because God raised
him from the dead (1.21). He is now the basis
of the spiritual household of God, but he is not
thereby any less alive.

The imagery here is complex. The point is that
Jesus is the centrepiece of God's plan to form a
people for himself: that is what it means when the
letter calls Jesus 'chosen' (2.6), which believers
are called to recognize (2.7). But the metaphor of
Jesus as a stone is also used to communicate that
he is offensive to some. Just as Jesus was rejected
by many of those to whom he ministered during
his earthly life, so too he is even now a 'stone
that makes [those who do not believe] stumble,
and a rock that makes them fall' (2.7–8, quoting
Ps. 118.22 and Isa. 8.14). Like a boulder in the
middle of a racecourse that can either be seen and
acknowledged or else tripped over and hated, so
Jesus is the cause of division: we can either trust

him and treat him as precious or else disbelieve and reject him.

Second, 1 Peter 2 depicts Jesus as united to believers. He is a 'living stone' and so are we: 'like living stones, let yourselves be built into a spiritual house' (2.5). Together, we are the dwelling of God. Jesus does not want to be without the Church. He is the head, and the Church is his body (see Eph. 4.15–16; Col. 1.18). In order to understand our identity and calling, we must look to his. And in order to understand how he saves us, we must grasp the indissoluble solidarity we now experience with him.

Third, 1 Peter 2 portrays Jesus as having suffered on our behalf: 'Christ ... suffered for you' (2.21). This means at least two things for Peter. On the one hand, it means that Jesus' suffering was in some mysterious way an exchange that allows us to experience blessing: 'He himself bore our sins in his body on the cross, so that, free from sins, we might live for righteousness; by his wounds you have been healed' (2.24). Jesus suffered as a substitute, so that we can now be granted life in place of death. On the other hand, Jesus' suffering on our behalf does not mean we are thereby exempt from having to suffer ourselves; Jesus left us 'an *example*, so that you should follow in his steps'

(2.21, emphasis added). As 1 Peter puts it later on, 'you are sharing Christ's sufferings, so that you may be glad and shout for joy when his glory is revealed' (4.13; see also Matt. 10.24–25; John 13.16; 15.20; Rom. 8.17).

Finally, 1 Peter 2 pictures Jesus as a shepherd. Although once we were far off from God, straying like a wayward flock, Jesus has gathered us back into the fold. This is one of the most beautiful images of Jesus that we find in the whole New Testament: Jesus is the 'shepherd and guardian of your souls' (2.25; see also John 10.11–13; Heb. 13.20; Rev. 7.17).

With all these images and themes in 1 Peter 2 – a living stone, the one who is in solidarity with us, our exchange (substitute) and example, and our shepherd – we can see more clearly who Jesus Christ is for us today.

1 Peter 2.4–10

4 Come to him, a living stone, though rejected by mortals yet chosen and precious in God's sight, and 5 like living stones, let yourselves be built into a spiritual house, to be a holy priesthood, to offer spiritual sacrifices acceptable to God through Jesus Christ. 6 For it stands in scripture:

'See, I am laying in Zion a stone,
    a cornerstone chosen and precious;
  and whoever believes in him will not be put to
    shame.'
[7] To you then who believe, he is precious; but for those who do not believe,
  'The stone that the builders rejected
    has become the very head of the corner',
[8] and
  'A stone that makes them stumble,
    and a rock that makes them fall.'
They stumble because they disobey the word, as they were destined to do.
[9] But you are a chosen race, a royal priesthood, a holy nation, God's own people, in order that you may proclaim the mighty acts of him who called you out of darkness into his marvellous light.
  [10] Once you were not a people,
      but now you are God's people;
    once you had not received mercy,
      but now you have received mercy.

A crucial section of this chapter is 1 Peter 2.4–10, as it describes traits that are key to the identity of Peter's listeners dwelling in a hostile society. The section is positioned at a critical juncture, sandwiched between Peter's exhortation that his listeners grow spiritually (2.1–3) and his account of the outworking of their

Christian identity in society (2.11–25). In 1 Peter 2.4–10, Peter uses a number of Old Testament texts to help articulate his understanding of his community's identity. One prominent example is his use of the 'rejected stone' motif, which alludes to Psalm 118.22 (1 Peter 2.4). In the Old Testament, the rejected stone refers to Israel who, though rejected by the nations, was accepted by God. In 1 Peter 2, however, the rejected stone – as expounded in the excursus above – refers directly to Christ.

According to M. Eugene Boring, there are three key themes in this section, all of which are related to the theme of Christian identity. The three themes are 1) the parallels between Christ and Christians; 2) the elaboration of the status of the elect; and 3) Christian mission of worship and testimony (Boring, pp. 96–102).

The parallels between Christ and Christians

In the face of a hostile society, the parallels between Christ and Christians are critical for Peter's understanding of Christian ethics. The status and behaviour of Christ are intended to evoke and give shape to an ethical response from the letter's recipients.

Peter affirms that both Christ and the letter's addressees are 'chosen' (2.4, 6, 9; see also 1.2 and note that this is 'elect' in some translations) and 'precious' (2.4, 6, 7; see also 1.7). His affirmations about Jesus thus serve to 'illuminate and provide the basis for his hearers' own Christian existence' (Boring, p. 97). That is to say, just as Jesus was rejected, Peter's listeners must not be surprised that they are being rejected. However, Jesus, the 'stone that the builders rejected, has become the very head of the corner' (2.7). And those who did not believe in this 'cornerstone' will stumble and fall (2.8). It's important to note that those who disobey the gospel in 2.8 are those who do not believe. They are not Christians and thus interpretations in the Church today must take care not to use this part of chapter 2 to address internal division.

Peter continues with a message of hope that his community should feel heartened that they will be vindicated in the last days because Jesus Christ has already been vindicated by God through the resurrection. The rejection and dishonour that Peter's listeners experience will be transformed to victory and honour, 'an honor they already experienced as the elect and holy people of God' (Boring, p. 97). In spite of opposition from society, Peter's community should find a sense of self-worth. They are the 'chosen' just as Christ is the 'chosen one'.

The status of those who are 'chosen'

The status of those who are 'chosen' – a status revisited at the very end of the letter – is explained in seven images. Each of the images is taken from the Old Testament where they apply to Israel. However, under Peter's pen, they are reapplied to his own community: the Church in the diaspora.

1 The first image is 'living stones' who are 'built into a spiritual house' (2.5). The only other passage in the letter where the term 'house' is used is 1 Peter 4.17, in which Christians are designated 'the household of God'. In the Old Testament, the 'house' of God referred to the 'temple', but the term is transferred to the Church in the New Testament. This term is reminiscent of Jesus' designation of Peter as the rock on which the Church would be built (see Matt. 16.16–18). In 1 Peter, the 'spiritual house' refers to the Christians, who are built on the foundation of Jesus who is the Rock (see 1 Peter 2.8). Thus, whatever the dispersion or division experienced by Christians, they are called to find a way to come together into a coherent building so that the Church does not crumble.

2 Another key image is 'holy priesthood' or 'royal priesthood' (2.5, 9). Those who are 'chosen' are also a holy and royal priesthood, an office which, in an Old Testament context, evoked the covenantal relationship between Israel and God (Ex. 19.6). This notion of covenantal relationship is carried over to the New Testament, in which that covenantal relationship binds the Christian

community to their God through God's Son, Jesus Christ. Furthermore, as a 'priesthood of believers', 1 Peter's recipients are to be a holy and intercessory community on behalf of the world.

3 A third image is 'chosen race'. The term 'chosen' is often translated as 'elect' and is applied to both Christ and Peter's community (1.2; 2.4, 6, 9; 5.13). It is the 'confessional language of the insiders who want to give praise to God for their being included, rather than taking credit for their own salvation' (Boring, p. 99).

4 'Holy nation' and 'God's own people' are two other pictures utilized to describe Peter's audience (2.9). The Greek terms translated 'nation' and 'people' communicate distinct ideas. In the plural form, the term 'nations' refers to the Gentiles, in contrast with the term which is translated as 'people' of God (for example Ex. 19.5; Deut. 7.6). The phrase rendered 'God's own people' (2.9) aims to communicate that the audience is a people who belong to God. Taking these references together, Peter is indicating that his listeners, be they Jewish or Gentiles, belonged to the economy of God's elect.

5 The last two pictures – 'people of God' and those who have 'received mercy' (2.10) – are taken from Hosea (1.6, 9–10; 2.23). In those Old Testament passages, the prophet contrasts adulterous Israel, who was being rejected by God, with the renewed Israel, which was

accepted by God. In characterizing the identity of Christians in these terms, Peter reminds his community that it was by God's initiative and mercy that they were accepted as God's own.

Peter's purpose in characterizing his listeners' identity with these affirmations is to sustain and encourage them so that they might proclaim the mighty acts of God who has 'called them out from darkness into [God's] marvellous light' (1 Peter 2.9). This brings us to the third theme of this section.

Christian mission of worship and testimony

Peter exhorts his community to bear witness in the world. He does not understand their identity in the rich theological terms outlined above simply in an effort to provide them with personal affirmation, but rather with the goal of moving them to bear witness, that is, 'to proclaim the mighty acts' of God (2.9). The nourishment they received from the 'spiritual milk' was not only to sustain them as followers of Jesus Christ but also to nurture them for mission. In the subsequent section, Peter begins to describe some examples of how his hearers should live and act in specific structures and contexts (2.11–25), especially when their identity is also connected to their status as outsider, exile and suffering.

Excursus: Communion

1 Peter does not offer an explicit discussion of communion. In fact, the letter opens by addressing the Church as something 'dispersed' or scattered, driven as 'exiles' around the world (1.1; 2.11). Yet in Peter's focus on the difficult realities of suffering and patient submission, and in the way these elements are linked to the identity of the Church as the chosen people of God, the reality of communion emerges in a striking and profound way. Communion is depicted as something that *emerges from* the common faithfulness of suffering discipleship.

A central theme in the letter is the way that suffering itself is caught up in a 'divine reversal'. This reversal is embodied in Jesus Christ himself as the 'rejected' stone who is then made the 'cornerstone' (2.4, 6, 7) and, as one suffering and killed, who is then raised up to God's right hand (3.17, 22). The Church, in its full life, is precisely built on this divine reversal, becoming the house constructed on the rejected stone (2.5). In this way, the Church stands in contrast to those who cannot receive or appreciate how God establishes that which human beings and human cultures deride and despise. The particularities of Christian calling – each disciple like a separate stone – are brought together into something whole simply in the common following of the rejected one in his humility and gentleness in the face of mistreatment and suffering (2.21–23).

Common suffering as disciples of Jesus, then, is *how* the Church is one, for it is the form of union with Christ himself, the realm in which his grace works to bring us to the fullness of salvation: 'But rejoice in so far as you are sharing [literally, 'have communion with'] Christ's sufferings, so that you may also rejoice and be glad and shout for joy when his glory is revealed' (4.13). Because Jesus himself brings salvation as a sheer act of 'mercy' (2.10) in the form of his own death for us (2.24; see also 1.2), divine grace does its transforming work as we come to look like him in this way. If communion reflects this reality of a common conformity to Christ, then communion is at the heart of the Church's identity.

There are some very concrete forms in which the Church's communion is thus lived out. These would come under the heading of faithfulness to Jesus' own 'way' embodied in his actions and words. In 1 Peter, this is described in terms of doing good (3.11), seeking peace and ordering life in a way that is not driven by inner passions or anger (2.11). This following in general implies even more specific forms of life among Christians, as they live within and before the world: treating one another in a way that is honest, charitable and always seeks the good of the other (2.1; see also 3.8–11; Col. 3.12–14). The Church's own life, among her members, takes the form of Jesus' own self-giving in love for the world. This means, finally, that the communion of the Church is itself embodied in the way members suffer the sins of others in patience, in the same way that Jesus suffers the sins of humanity on the cross: 'Above all, maintain constant love for one another, for love covers a multitude of sins. Be hospitable to one another without complaining' (4.8–9; see also 1.22; 3.8–9).

The challenges for the global church are various: evangelistic integrity and energy in the face of apathy or denials of the gospel; addressing the burdens of poverty suffered by member churches, peoples, or whole nations; labouring under, exposing and rooting out corruption within church and civil society; and, of course, ongoing and diminishing conflicts over sexuality. Peter's letter shows that Christian communion is not so much the result of resolving these challenges successfully, as it is the 'way' such challenges are to be engaged together: with mutual love, in humility and gentleness, and with ungrudging hospitality.

Having articulated the basics of Christian identity and existence, Peter now shifts towards social responsibility. This section could also be divided into two subsections: a general introduction about public conduct, especially in relationship to governmental structures (2.11–17), and a section on the conduct of slaves, viewed in the light of Christ's own suffering (2.18–25). As stated at the start of this chapter, neither of these subsections can be separated from the summons at the start of chapter 3.

---

1 Peter 2.11–17

[11] Beloved, I urge you as aliens and exiles to abstain from the desires of the flesh that wage war against the soul. [12] Conduct yourselves honourably among the Gentiles, so that, though they malign you as evildoers, they may see your honourable deeds and glorify God when he comes to judge. [13] For the Lord's sake accept the authority of every human institution, whether of the emperor as supreme, [14] or of governors, as sent by him to punish those who do wrong and to praise those who do right. [15] For it is God's will that by doing right you should silence the ignorance of the foolish. [16] As servants of God, live as free people, yet do not use your freedom as a pretext for evil. [17] Honour everyone. Love the family of believers. Fear God. Honour the emperor.

Verses 11–12 connect with the argument of the previous section about the true identity of the believer (2.9–10). The difference of the believing community is emphasized in 2.9: 'a peculiar people' as the King James version appropriately puts it. But now Peter introduces another aspect of the identity of his community, that of being 'aliens and exiles'. As 'aliens and exiles' Peter's listeners are warned that they should not conform to the social and religious norms of society that were contradictory to Jesus Christ, to whom they pledged their allegiance (2.11). They are pushed towards the recognition of one 'Lord' in tension with other 'lords' in the world around them.

At the same time, however, Peter does not ask his community to withdraw from society. They are to engage constructively with the Gentiles so as not to evoke suspicion but instead, by their witness, to move the Gentiles to give honour to God for the 'honourable deeds' of the Christians. The 'honourable deeds' to which the believers are called include abstinence from the 'desires of the flesh'. Put differently, they should not return to the immoral behaviours of their former lives but should live up to the noblest aspirations of Roman morality. While this reference to Roman morality may seem surprising to twenty-first-century Christian readers who often think of ancient Romans and Greeks as being wicked or licentious, it bears remembering that there were also moral Romans living in Asia

Minor (Boring, p. 114), some of whom suspected that the Christians were immoral. The righteous conduct of Peter's listeners, therefore, was to assuage the suspicions of their pagan neighbours and to bear witness to God. Thus, the practice of a good way of life, shaped both inwardly and outwardly by doing good, will have an impact on those who misrepresent Peter's community as evildoers.

The final few words of 2.12, emphasizing God as judge, clearly stresses the tension in the relationship between the community of believers and the dominant world and makes clear who is ultimate lord and judge. In the verses that follow, Peter gives specific examples as to how his community could, on the one hand, demonstrate their 'alienated' status and, on the other hand, bear witness to God. For this purpose, Peter takes up the topic of governmental authority.

In 2.13–17 Peter instructs his hearers to be subject to all *human* institutions, especially the 'emperors' or 'governors sent by him' (see also Rom. 13.1–10). The force of the verb in 2.13 might range from a strong sense of 'submit' to a weak sense of 'accept' (or 'tolerate'). How we understand the verb 'accept the authority of' depends largely on how we understand the phrase 'for the Lord's sake' at the start, which motivates the action. The logic so far suggests that the value of such acceptance is not because of any core value in these human authority structures, but because such an acceptance will give pause to those who are slandering God's people and accusing them of evildoing. Thus, within this section and the following one (from 2.18), Peter uses the Hellenist moral tradition of 'household management' to address the subject of social order, that is, what it means to conduct oneself 'honourably among the Gentiles' (2.12).

Societies at the time 1 Peter was written were greatly concerned with the establishment and maintenance of 'order' in all areas of life, private and public included. At the top of Roman social order were the emperor and other political leaders, such as the senators and governors. In relation to such figures, Peter commands his listeners to 'accept the authority' of them. Although human rulers were, at their best, capable of doing the divine work of punishing injustice and protecting the righteous, Peter's community would have understood that human authorities did not have ultimate claims upon them (especially when they became agents of injustice), since the Christian's allegiance ultimately is to Jesus Christ. Nonetheless, because in the best of cases governing authorities could be agents of God's justice and serve the healthy order of society, Christians are urged to submit to their governors, not as a matter of compulsion or fatalism, but 'for the Lord's sake' (2.13).

It's worth pondering the possibility that 1 Peter may be offering a deliberately ambiguous argument in 2.13–14. We could read these verses as arguing

that accepting the authority of the emperor and
his governors is part of God's order (God does the
sending). Or, we could read these verses as arguing
that accepting the authority of the emperor and his
governors is (merely) part of the dominant human
order (the emperor does the sending). The difference
is significant. Such ambiguity is a characteristic of
literature aimed at those who are marginalized,
outsiders, aliens. Those of the dominant order – the
emperor or his governors – who might intercept
such literature would understand one thing, while
the intended recipients would hear something quite
different.

The doing of right (2.14, 15) may also mean
something quite different. Within the dominant
order of empire (2.12), doing right is focused on
receiving 'praise' from the rulers of that order. For
those who are part of God's chosen people, doing
right is not so much about eliciting the praise of
the system, but about silencing 'the ignorance of the
foolish' (2.15). There is an implicit critique here of
the dominant empire – 'of every human institution'
(2.13) – characterized as it is by 'the ignorance of
the foolish'.

Peter transitions from the language of living
under empire to urge his hearers as 'servants of
God' to 'live as free people' (2.16), clarifying that
they must exercise their freedom responsibly within
the structures of the society. There is a strategic
submission to the order of the empire in this section,

but here the essential submission is to God. Even so, this primary submission cannot be used as an excuse for evil. Peter's instructions do not include a collection of dos and don'ts. More concisely, he exhorts his community to act in good conscience. Since these governmental authorities were installed for the purpose of punishing those who did evil, those who did good should have nothing to fear.

This section of 1 Peter 2 climaxes with some key reminders to Peter's recipients, making the priorities and distinctions of his community clear. While everyone was to be honoured, including the emperor (which in itself could be seen as a subversive flattening of Roman hierarchy, placing the emperor on the same level as 'everyone'), it is only God that they were to fear (2.17) and the community of believers that they are to love. 'Honour' as an outward virtue is appropriate for all and the emperor; 'love' as an inner virtue is required for the community of believers; and 'fear' (or awe) is the appropriate stance towards God. For Peter, in contrast to the honour that is due to all, 'fear/reverence is reserved for God alone and [in this letter, fear] is more prominent as a motivation for exhortation (1.17; 3.2, 6, 14, 16) than in any New Testament writing' (Elliot 2000, p. 500, citing Goppelt, p. 190).

The letter then turns to two dominant systems of human institutions: slavery (2.18–25) and patriarchy (3.1–7). Slavery and patriarchy are the two most prevalent and enduring systems of the ancient world, so widespread that they are all but invisible. Remarkably, this letter makes them visible.

Excursus: Christian Ethics in Canonical Context

Above the Great Western Door of Westminster Abbey stand ten statues of twentieth-century martyrs. Exemplars of unwavering Christian commitment in the face of injustice, most of these saints – Oscar Romero, Martin Luther King Jr, Maximilian Kolbe, Janani Luwum, Wang Zhiming, Elizabeth of Hesse,. Dietrich Bonhoeffer – lost their lives precisely for resisting the evil policies and practices of their nations and leaders. Yet, when one strolls backwards a bit, the iconic towers of Westminster Palace come into view behind the Abbey, a reminder that the Church of England is the established church of its country. How does one hold together the martyrs' legacy of resistance to evil governments with an equally robust history of Christian churches allying themselves constructively with worldly nations? Are both these postures compatible, across the spectrum of the global Christian church and in relation to the biblical witness?

In point of fact, Christian scriptures generate, justify and sustain both these relationships with governments. On the one hand, 1 Peter exhorts believers, 'For the Lord's sake accept the authority of every human institution, whether of the emperor as supreme, or of governors, as sent by him to punish those who do wrong and to praise those who do right' (1 Peter 2.13–14); the apostle Paul similarly instructs,

> Let every person be subject to the governing authorities; for there is no authority except from God, and those authorities that exist have been instituted by God ... For rulers are not a terror to good conduct, but to bad ... For [the government] is God's servant for your good. (Rom. 13.1–4)

On the other hand, the book of Revelation depicts the same Roman Empire as a woman riding on a seven-headed, ten-horned beast, calling her 'mother of horrors and of Earth's abominations' and describing her as 'drunk with the blood of the saints and the blood of the witnesses to Jesus' (Rev. 17.6). In this, the Seer follows the example of the book of Daniel, which also described a contemporary nation as a terrifying beast with ten horns that 'made war with the holy ones' (Dan. 7.19–27, citing v. 21). Thus, the biblical canon provides precedents for both positive Christian submission to governors as servants of God and faithful Christian resistance to human states as agents of the devil. (Admittedly, Christians – even the martyrs mentioned above – have historically had dramatically different views of God and *how* appropriately to resist the unjust State; contrast the passivism of Martin Luther King Jr with Bonhoeffer's failed conspiracy to assassinate Hitler.) Does this mean, however, that the Bible is insuperably self-contradictory and therefore offers little reliable guidance to struggling communities of faith?

Quite the contrary, actually. The range of the biblical canon's witness on Church–State relations reflects the diversity of the historical contexts in which God inspired the biblical authors. Both 1 Peter and Paul's letter to the Romans were drafted during times when the Roman Empire was not actively hostile to Christians, even though some of the Christians' fellow subjects in the Empire were indeed persecuting believers. As such, the biblical authors exhorted their readers to remain irreproachable in their relationship to the State, such that the government might come to their protection rather than having reason to side with their opponents. Thus, the government could function as a servant of the Lord on behalf of the saints. Conversely, the book of Revelation was likely drafted under the reign of Domitian, one of the few first-century Roman emperors to institute official imperial persecution of believers. Accordingly, the Seer warns his audiences that the current Roman administration was doing the will, not of God, but the devil, which entailed suffering and martyrdom for the faithful who would not blithely submit to or collude with the evil actions of their rulers.

In this way, the revelatory diversity of the canon mirrors the different historical moments in and through which God guided his people. This canonical diversity is not limited to the witness of the scriptures regarding governments, but also applies to the scriptures' teachings on matters of violence (within the same Gospel, contrast Matt. 5.5–9, 21–22, 38–39, 43–45; 7.12; 22.39–40; 26.51–52; with Matt. 10.34–36; 21.12–13, 40–41; 22.7; 24.48–51), gender (compare, for example, Gen. 3.6; Judg. 4.4; Rom. 16.7; 1 Cor. 11.3; 14.34–35; Gal. 3.28; 1 Tim. 2.9–15) and money (examine, for example, Gen. 13.2; Deut. 28.11–12; 2 Chron. 1.11–12; Prov. 3.9–10; Mal. 3.10; Matt. 19.21; Luke 6.20, 24; 14.33; James 5.1–3). This requires, therefore, that the Church's pastors and leaders be wise interpreters – not only of the biblical text in its many canonical facets, embedded in distinct historical contexts, but also of their own historical context – asking what God, who is revealed in Christ and in the scriptures, wills in relation to their own nation and culture, all the while recognizing that the same God and the same scriptures may speak differently and truly to their sisters and brothers guided by the Spirit elsewhere on the globe.

1 Peter 2.18–25

[18] Slaves, accept the authority of your masters with all deference, not only those who are kind and gentle but also those who are harsh. [19] For it is to your credit if, being aware of God, you endure pain while suffering unjustly. [20] If you endure when you are beaten for doing wrong, where is the credit in that? But if you endure when you do right and suffer for it, you have God's approval. [21] For to this you have been called, because Christ also suffered for you, leaving you an example, so that you should follow in his steps. [22] 'He committed no sin, and no deceit was found in his mouth.' [23] When he was abused, he did not return abuse; when he suffered, he did not threaten; but he entrusted himself to the one who judges justly. [24] He himself bore our sins in his body on the cross, so that, free from sins, we might live for righteousness; by his wounds you have been healed. [25] For you were going astray like sheep, but now you have returned to the shepherd and guardian of your souls.

There is an abrupt shift, or so it would seem, from the slightly subversive tone of 2.13–17 to the opening phrase of 2.18, 'Slaves, accept the authority of'. Peter moves to what is known as the 'household code', which is instruction to the whole Church with respect to the conduct of slaves, wives and husbands (see also Eph. 5.21–6.9; Col. 3.18–4.1). The first group addressed is slaves.

In the Graeco–Roman world, slaves were major contributors to the economy of the empire, since they acted as labourers for many of the empire's households. Slaves were procured as a result of warfare, the inability to pay one's debt, birth into slavery, or abduction. Additionally, voluntary enslavement was sometimes utilized as a strategy to acquire citizenship. But slaves themselves did not have citizenship rights and, therefore, could be ill-treated, separated from their families, and were ranked on the bottom rung of the social hierarchy, with no honour or means of support except from their owners (Elliot 2000, p. 514). Within this context, it is worth noting that the letter addresses the slaves directly. They are the subjects of this section. We might expect to hear an allusion to Exodus 3, to God who hears the cry of slaves and those in exile. But there God summoned Moses to lead a rebellion. Here in 1 Peter, the summons is different.

As attentive readers we are expected to recognize the tension within the letter at this point. 'God's own people' have just been told in 2.16 that they must 'live as free people' in a mutual relationship of love among the community of believers (2.17). Yet now, some of the family of believers are singled out for special instructions. And what follows is disturbing. For having just been told that 'fear' is reserved for God alone (2.17), this particular sector of 'God's own people' must 'accept the authority of your masters with all deference' (2.18). How are we to understand the coherence of 1 Peter at this point?

One way of understanding 2.18 in relation to all that has gone before is to recognize with the apostolic author just how precarious life is for the slaves who are part of the community of believers. Because they serve two masters – the slave-master and God – there is a dangerous tension at the very core of their lives. Because they are members of 'God's chosen people' and members of the system of slavery, they live with an unbearable reality, both free in Christ and slaves in the Graeco–Roman system. And Scripture offers multiple trajectories with respect to such tensions, ranging from overt resistance to the dominant system (Ex. 3) to conformity to the dominant order (Rom. 13).

In the exhortation to the slaves within his community of faith, 1 Peter errs on the side of survival. Resistance to powerful and deep-rooted systems, such as slavery, could well lead to death. The letter counsels survival and thus 'doing good' within the system in order to survive the system. Survival is key, the letter argues, in conjunction with the forging of a theological resilience which in God's time will enable the alienated and exiled believer to speak back to power. A tension is held within 1 Peter between how to be faithful and how to survive.

In contrast to other 'household codes' in the New Testament, where slaves are the last group to be addressed, in 1 Peter 2 slaves are mentioned first. In this way, Peter effectively construes 'household slaves as paradigms for the entire household of faith' (Elliot 2000, p. 514), most likely because slaves often suffered unjustly, just as Christ did and just as other Christians in Peter's community did. The slaves addressed in this household code are viewed and treated as 'responsible members of the inclusive Christian community' (Boring, p.117), although they could be slaves of non-Christian masters since the letter makes no mention of the obligations of Christian masters towards slaves. These slaves were marginalized and vulnerable, not only because of their legal status just described, but also because slaves were often looked upon as thieves, liars and slackers. However, Peter speaks directly to them and urges them to continue to do good in spite of being wrongly accused (2.19–20).

These exhortations then of Christians to honour the emperor while fearing God and of Christian slaves not to respond in sin when treated unjustly, hold before us the vulnerability of most Christians in the first century, who were on the margins. It confirms for us what Peter means when he calls his community 'aliens and exiles'. Such realities serve both to encourage Christians today who find themselves in positions of persecution and marginalization and to remind Christians living in a dominant Christian society not to grow too comfortable or be lulled into complacency. An awareness of how easily one can become vulnerable to systems of power within the ancient world, and still in our world today, is one we cannot neglect.

The juxtaposition of 2.13–17 and 2.18–25 demonstrates Peter's awareness of the theological tension he is trying to navigate. Survival in such circumstances, being both free in Christ and a slave within the dominant Graeco–Roman economic system, is a daily struggle. Being an object (a slave) for one who is a subject (God's own person) requires a particular form of discipline. The letter understands this, particularly when masters are not 'kind and gentle' but 'harsh' (2.18). Surviving a 'kind and gentle' master is difficult for those who are free men and women, but surviving a harsh master is dangerous.

No explanation is given for their unjust suffering, nor does Peter call for slaves to resist and get justice for themselves. However, this silence surely is not because of any indifference about injustice, but rather the apostolic author's awareness that the powerless slaves were not in a position to secure such justice on their own behalf. Thus, they were left with the choice of responding sinfully to their suffering, or responding with righteous endurance and resilience, knowing that they thereby honoured God and imitated Christ. It warrants underscoring that this exhortation to endure was not aimed at the slaves only; it applies rather to all the addressees of this letter, since they were also suffering. In order to support his call for patient endurance and perseverance in righteousness without any retaliation, Peter cites the image of Christ as the suffering servant of Isaiah 53, who effectively becomes a model for all his followers (Horrell 2008, pp. 63–5).

Therefore, the theological line the letter takes in encouraging resilience is to align the unjust suffering of those who are doing right with the unjust suffering of Christ (2.19–23). The apostolic author clarifies that Christ's suffering is not merely a historical fact, but an example for the listeners and readers of the letter who are to 'follow in his steps' (2.21). In his suffering on behalf of others, Jesus demonstrated submission to and trust in God. He suffered shame and death on the cross but was vindicated by God for his uprightness. Christ sets the example of unjust suffering (2.22–23), an example that slaves are called to follow (2.21). Peter recognizes that suffering unjustly requires resilience: to patiently endure (2.20, twice). Resilience, patient endurance, in the face of unjust suffering meets 'God's approval' (2.20).

What is more, the suffering of Christ was for the benefit of sinful humanity; 'he himself bore our sins in his body on the cross' (2.24; see also Phil. 2.6–11), and the forgiveness Jesus offers results in freedom from the power of sin, which in turn enables Christians to live righteously amid a world of wickedness. Thus, Jesus not only left his followers an example, teaching them to endure suffering in a God-honouring fashion; but by freeing them from the power of sin, he also enabled them to endure suffering and to live justly in the midst of injustice.

The conjunction 'but' is key to the logic of the argument that follows from 2.21 in how to live justly in the midst of injustice. There may not be justice in the dominant world, but there is justice in the world God will bring about. Resilience is possible in the face of unjust suffering at the hands of slave-masters because God is a just judge. Justice will, the letter assures slaves, be done. The writer of 1 Peter accepts, it would seem, that the system of slavery must be endured if a Church consisting partly of slaves is to survive. Resisting slavery would result in the destruction of the Church. The beautifully crafted letter of Paul to Philemon, on behalf of the slave Onesimus, is a clear example of how careful even Paul is about being overtly condemnatory about slavery as a system. The advantage Paul has is that Philemon, the slave-master, is a fellow believer, but even in that case, Paul is tactful in the way he encourages Philemon to consider freeing Onesimus. By contrast, 1 Peter addresses the slaves themselves, not the slave-masters.

The theological argument of 1 Peter in its addressing of slaves in the community of faith does not end in verse 23. Christ's example of resilient endurance in the face of systemic unjust suffering is a real example of an actual lived reality. Such is the affirmation of 2.23. But 2.24 takes the argument to another level. Taking a Paul-like turn, 1 Peter offers slaves a further resource on which to draw in their patient suffering as they continue to do good within a system that refuses to recognize God's just order. Christ's unjust suffering has already accomplished justice, freedom from sins and healing. Here, as elsewhere in the letter, the scriptures are invoked (Isa. 53.5) to offer comfort: 'by his wounds you have been healed' (2.24). A life of resilient righteousness following the example of Christ, leads to healing which can only be found in Christ.

Peter concludes this section with the image of the shepherd and the sheep. He reminds his community that they were once straying sheep who had been brought back by the shepherd who laid down his life for his sheep (see also John 10.11–18) and was now the 'guardian of [their] souls' (2.25). Even as they endure suffering, they are being watched over, contended for, by the shepherd who knew full well what it was to endure injustice and who would indeed vindicate their suffering, just as the Father had vindicated him. This image of shepherd will return to the front of Peter's exhortation and his understanding of Christ in chapter 5.

Questions for reflection

1   1 Peter describes the people of God both as 'aliens and exiles' and as chosen, and says that because of this, Christians will suffer.
    • What does it mean to suffer for Christ?
    • How can we walk together with those who, to us, are alien and exile?
    • What would it look like to love them as a chosen person of God?
    • What role can the Church play in a world that seeks to fragment and divide?

2   1 Peter calls followers of Christ to be living stones, built up into a spiritual house.
    • What does this call in 2.4–5 mean for you? For your church community?

3   1 Peter speaks about 'accepting the authority' of the empire or government while at the same time asserting an identity connected to Christ in this world.
    • When has your faith put you in conflict with your government?
    • How does 1 Peter teach us to stand up against injustice when complaining and protesting are not options?
    • What good deeds might you do that can change someone or a system?

When has your faith put you in conflict with the church?

- How do you witness to Christ within structures of power?

4 Peter also writes about systems of oppression in our world, using slavery and empire as examples in this chapter. *Church? Balla supporters*
- What passages in 1 Peter have been misused in our world to justify oppression and injustice?
- How do you resist oppression in your community? In your world?

5 When it comes to sin, we are sometimes more open to some sins than others, for example we might condemn slavery but not empire.
- Where do we live with structures of oppression?
- Where are we complicit with structural sins that create more strangers and exiles?
- What sins do we judge rather than leaving judgement to Christ, the just judge and shepherd and guardian of souls?

3

Resistance and Resilience in Christ (1 Peter 3)

'Into Bondage' (1936), Aaron Douglas.

'Into Bondage': in this painting, Aaron Douglas uses chains and ships to evoke the shameful history of the enslavement of Africans. But, notwithstanding the chains, this painting contains hope and commemorates the contribution of African and African American strength and culture to the eventual abolition of slavery. The woman in the bottom left corner raises her bound hands; the man on the auction block in the centre stands tall and raises his head to the light emanating from a star. The circles, radiating from the horizon, represent the songs (spirituals) of coded resistance sung by African American slaves. We are all encouraged in 1 Peter to live as a free people whatever our circumstances – a freedom based on our relationship with Christ.

Aaron Douglas, African American artist, used by permission of DACS

Chapter 3 of Peter's first letter begins with an immediate link to 1 Peter 2, starting with the words 'in the same way'. As mentioned in the introduction and at the start of the previous chapter, the divisions of 1 Peter are not that helpful. With the phrase 'in the same way' drawing on the instructions Peter has just given concerning slaves, 2.13–25 cannot be separated from the start of 1 Peter 3. The calls to various sectors of the Church to 'accept the authority of' (2.13, 18; 3.1) belong together. Peter is asking his community to think in all these cases about what it means to acknowledge authority, to submit, to honour, and how to return good for evil as a pattern that instructs all Christians in conformity to Christ, who suffered sometimes without a word and yet remains victor in that submission. An understanding of the letter's argument, therefore, requires locating the three summonses to 'accept the authority of ...' within a section that includes (at least) 2.11–3.7, as well as 3.8–17 and particularly 3.15.

1 Peter 3.8–17 is included because these verses offer the essential support for a theological ethic that frames and interprets 2.11–3.7. The pivotal component of the support is the call to 'in your hearts sanctify Christ as Lord' (3.15). This crucial call summons the community of 1 Peter to frame the earlier calls to 'accept the authority of' in relationship to, perhaps even in tension with, the ultimate Lordship of Christ. Thus 3.8–17 requires hard interpretive work from the reader of this letter. How are we to understand the relationship between 'the Lord' and the many other claims to lordship of that time, including the lordship of 'human institutions' (2.13), 'masters' (2.18) and 'husbands' (3.1)? And how is sanctifying Christ as Lord in our hearts an act both of resilience and of resistance in a world of lord-less powers?

Framing the argument with respect to the three forms of human authority using 3.15 provides a way of understanding an important tension or continuum that Peter is grappling with. Given the demands of competing claims of 'lordship', how should Christians behave, particularly when, as in the case of Peter's community, Christians are a marginalized and vulnerable community? Furthermore, how are contemporary Christians in very different contexts, especially those in which Christianity is or has been a dominant religious tradition, to understand the message of 1 Peter?

The response of 1 Peter to the very real contest among 'lords' in the world of those who 'sojourn in a strange place' (1.1) could be understood along a continuum, ranging from conformity, to resilience, to resistance. At one end of the continuum is an implied resistance to other lords because Christ is the only true Lord. The call from 1 Peter here is to a resistance enabling resilience in the face of systems of dominance. At the other end of the continuum there is the theological assumption that an 'acceptance' of the Lordship of Christ requires as an essential element the 'acceptance' of these other forms of lordship. The call from the letter at this end of the continuum is to a recognition of aligned kindred lordships. The letter offers less a clear-cut resolution of this tension than an array of resources for grappling, theologically and practically, with a real socio-historical predicament and its attendant challenges.

Our contemporary locations in the world and the perspectives that shape our Christian witness will of course shape where we as readers lean or err along this continuum. For example, resistance and resilience are held together in some parts of our world where it is illegal to build churches and yet Christian communities continue to build new buildings, and in those buildings pray for the ruler whose rules make such a space illegal.

In what follows we pay careful attention to the textual detail of 3.1–7, with an eye always to 2.11–

25 in an attempt to discern what resources the text offers the reader who is faithfully navigating this continuum.

> ## 1 Peter 3.1–7
>
> [1] Wives, in the same way, accept the authority of your husbands, so that, even if some of them do not obey the word, they may be won over without a word by their wives' conduct, [2] when they see the purity and reverence of your lives. [3] Do not adorn yourselves outwardly by braiding your hair, and by wearing gold ornaments or fine clothing; [4] rather, let your adornment be the inner self with the lasting beauty of a gentle and quiet spirit, which is very precious in God's sight. [5] It was in this way long ago that the holy women who hoped in God used to adorn themselves by accepting the authority of their husbands. [6] Thus Sarah obeyed Abraham and called him lord. You have become her daughters as long as you do what is good and never let fears alarm you. [7] Husbands, in the same way, show consideration for your wives in your life together, paying honour to the woman as the weaker sex, since they too are also heirs of the gracious gift of life – so that nothing may hinder your prayers.

Rather oddly, at some moment in 1 Peter's history in the 1500s, a chapter break was inserted at the start of this section, separating slaves from wives. While we might speculate about the theological agenda that inserted itself into the letter via the chapter division at this time, we can be sure that the early hearers of the letter would recognize that the theological logic that was used with respect to slaves is similar to that used with respect to wives who are both called to 'accept the authority of'.

Indeed, it is important for contemporary readers of 1 Peter not to pause at the end of the second chapter. We must grapple theologically with a text from Scripture that uses the same kind of theological argument for slaves and women/wives. In the ancient world slaves and women occupied a similar social status, as objects of elite men. There are parts of our contemporary world where little has changed. There are also parts of our world in which the system of slavery has been rejected by the Church, but not the system of patriarchy. And there are parts of our world in which both systems have been rejected. Such divergent contexts will mean people approaching 1 Peter quite differently when it comes to a contemporary appropriation of this Scripture.

The text is clear, both in terms of the link between those under human institutions, slaves and wives, and in what the wives are to do. The text of 3.1 begins with the adverb 'in the same way' which is directly connected to the now familiar verb 'accept the authority of'. The subject of this similar instruction is 'women', though it soon becomes clear that the primary focus is married women. For 1 Peter, married women are like slaves. The shape of the argument is also similar, as befits the common status of slaves and women in the Graeco–Roman world. Neither slaves nor women had power, a status that fits well into the wider community of 1 Peter since we must remember that aliens and exiles do not have any power either.

Though the reader should *not* pause here in terms of the theological argument, the combination of an address to these two sectors, slaves and wives, does warrant a pause. What the combination makes clear is that these two sectors form a substantial part of the community of faith, of 'the people of God' (2.10) to whom 1 Peter is addressed. How remarkable that such a substantive part of the community of faith is made up of those of low social status.

The question the letter continues to grapple with in this third section is how do those who are required 'to accept the authority of' the dominant systems of the day, slavery and patriarchy, reconcile this submission with the call to 'sanctify Christ as Lord' (3.15)? Again, the letter could be arguing that the Church must conform itself to the dominant order of the ruling system. It has certainly been read in this way. But the letter can also be read as a recognition of a contest between lordships, cautioning those who are objects of slavery and patriarchy to accept these systems in order to survive and so to give themselves the opportunity of testifying to God's alternative order (3.15).

Excursus: Identity and the Church

Within 1 Peter, the Church is described as having a clear identity as royal priesthood, holy nation, a special people with a specific calling to praise God before creation (2.9). This identity subsumes the many identities noted throughout the letter – of citizens, servants, masters, wives, husbands, older and younger persons, as well as of various ministries (4.10). The full variety of lives and stations, in their scattered and often difficult experience, is here gathered and 'built' together in a common reality (2.5). The letter explains 'God's chosen people' in terms of a concrete set of relationships of service, relationships that come down to a form of life: Jesus' suffering for others, which marks out the path that the Church's special people is to 'follow' (2.21).

'Following' is among the most common words used to describe the disciples in the Gospels. Right from the start of his ministry (see also Mark 1.18), those who join Jesus are said to have left behind what they were doing and 'followed' him. Peter tells us that this call to follow Jesus, in a very real way, is given to all Christians (2.9; see also 5.10). The letter, furthermore, makes clear that following is not a general theory, nor is it an aimless passage. Rather, the following of the Church is tied to the 'footsteps' of Jesus, along a path that we know from the Gospels in retrospect, and that the scriptures more broadly explicate (see also Luke 24.25–27).

The writer of 1 Peter emphasizes the sheer privilege or grace of following Jesus' steps: the Church and her members have been granted the favour to know *him* (1.2, 10–12); they have been allowed to share (be in 'communion' with) his way (4.13); and they are being taken to his destination of glory (1.7; 4.13). In other words, this is all a gift from God that we should be joined to God's own life. That life stands as 'light' and the fullness of human personhood and corporate integrity.

The grace of following takes the form of an array of acts, according to 1 Peter, lived out in relation to other people: truthfulness, purity, openness, honesty, charity, the search for agreement, compassion, courtesy, forgiveness, blessing (1.22; 2.1; 3.8–9). These acts, simply in their pursuit, bring suffering upon believers, so that the divine love that animates them all can be summarized in terms of 'endurance' (2.19) and 'humility' (5.5). Such

> patience and humility, lived out among the
> followers of Christ, *is* the holy nation of the Church.
> The Church's identity as the people of God, then,
> consists of following the footsteps of Christ.

The chapter break between the section on 'slaves'
and 'wives' might indicate an awareness, already in
the 1500s, that while an argument could be made
for an alignment between the cultural norms of the
1500s and the Graeco–Roman context of 1 Peter
with respect to patriarchy, such an argument was
more difficult to sustain with respect to slavery. In
many parts of the contemporary world, including
many parts of the global church, such a distinction
is made and practised. The system of slavery is
seen as part of the ancient world, a system that
must be rejected in contemporary contexts by
Christians. However, the system of patriarchy is
maintained by many Christians – both in general
and in the submission of women to their husbands
in particular as part of God's enduring order –
aligning contemporary socio-cultural norms with
ancient socio-cultural norms and so sanctifying
them. But 1 Peter will not allow us to make this
distinction. Slavery and patriarchy are 'similar'.

With respect to wives, 1 Peter follows a similar
logic to the previous sections on empire and slavery.
Wives are to be submissive to their 'husbands' (3.1),
not because such submission is a virtue in itself,

but for a distinct purpose: 'so that, even if some of them do not obey the word (*logos*), they may be won over without a word (*logos*) by their wives' conduct'. There is perhaps a hint of humour in the play on the word 'word'. It may have been the case that within the community of faith these women were 'free people' (2.16) when it came to speaking within the community of faith. But Peter recognizes that wives who are too vocal at home in engaging their husbands about their life of faith might be seen as transgressing the socio-cultural norms of the household. If the Word is to prevail it must be without words! But, as the wives will hear a little later in this chapter, they must 'always be ready to make your defence to anyone who demands from you an account (literally: to give a word [*logos*]) for the hope that is in you; yet do it with gentleness and reverence' (3.15–16). Wordless witness to the Word, Jesus, will enable a word to be spoken. Wordless submission is not a virtue in itself; it is a missional strategy.

As we have already discussed in Chapter 2, resistance to powerful and deep-rooted systems, such as slavery and patriarchy, could lead to death. Slaves who resist their masters and wives who resist their husbands risk death. Peter's letter counsels survival, 'doing what is good' (3.6; cf. 2.20) within the system in order to survive the system. Survival is key, it is argued, for it enables the forging of a resilience that in God's time will enable the alienated and exiled believer to speak back to power. Wives, it would seem, are under surveillance (3.2), and so Peter wants to ensure that those watching with evil intent (2.12) should observe 'the purity and reverence' of their lives (3.2). What is not clear, and what may be deliberately ambiguous (again), is whether it is God or the husband who is the primary observer. Fear, we have encountered (2.17), is primarily associated with the believer's relationship with God. Perhaps here, as with slaves (2.18), husbands are only secondary observers of behaviour that is primarily a product of these women's relationship with God.

We can certainly understand the instructions that follow in this way, for in 3.3–4 it is clear that the ordering of these women is to be shaped not by an 'outwardly' order of contemporary fashion, whether hair, jewellery, or clothing (3.3), but by 'the inner self' characterized by the lasting virtues of 'a gentle and quiet spirit' (3.4). Though the virtues are ancient qualities associated particularly with women, what is somewhat subversive is that Peter here acknowledges and affirms that the women being addressed have a 'hidden' identity that is lived out primarily 'in God's sight' (3.4), not that of their husbands. As with slaves, the writer is urging godly virtues in order to survive ungodly husbands. God is the focus, not the husbands.

Perhaps the same logic of resilience is present too in the reference to precedent for this behaviour (3.5–6). The repetition of the phrase 'accept the authority of their/your husbands' (3.1, 5) recognizes the constraints of the ancient world on women. Women belonged to their husbands. Peter recognizes this cultural reality, but seems to subvert it as well. He reminds these women that even though their ancestor Sarah was as culturally constrained as they are, she lived her life by another order, 'hoping in God' (3.5) even as she 'obeyed Abraham and called him lord' (3.6). Peter is clear, these women are not to be ordered or intimidated by their husbands, rather they are to 'do what is good' in the sight of God and 'never let fears alarm you' (3.6).

The letter now turns to 'husbands' (3.7). The force of the repetition of 'in the same way' suggests that there is, once again, a similar logic or argument here. If Peter is exhorting this marginalized community to live resilient ways of life that enable survival in a world that watches them with evil intent, then here too we might discern a call to forms of faith that do not overtly resist the dominant order. This is also a call that summons the believer to trust that by ordering their lives in God's sight, they will survive and even have the opportunity to witness and give an account for the hope that is in them.

The exhortation to 'husbands' is to 'show consideration for your wives in your life together'. Here, the term for 'consideration' is the same as that for 'knowledge' and may well convey the 'experiential knowledge' of having to navigate a world in which they are 'exiles and aliens' (2.11).

Husbands are exhorted to recognize that women generally and their own wives in particular are the 'weaker sex' (literally: 'vulnerable bodies') in this alien world, and so to 'pay honour' to their wives who are 'also heirs of the gracious gift of life' in God (3.7). They must do what the dominant order does not do and thus also subvert the system in their 'paying honour' to women.

The apostolic author ends with a warning to 'husbands'. If they do not follow this godly way of life, but instead conform to the way of life of the dominant powers, they face the danger of disruption in their relationship with God, the risk that they 'may hinder your prayers' (3.7). For 1 Peter, a right relationship with God requires a right relationship with women.

Submission to the systems of the dominant order, whether to emperors, governors, slave-masters, or husbands, should not be understood as having an intrinsic value. Submission to these powerful systems is strategic for mission, a by-product of the ultimate submission which is to God. By 'sanctifying Christ as Lord' in their hearts, they will have opportunities to give 'an account of the hope' that resides in them (3.15).

Excursus: The Dangers and Misuse of 1 Peter 2–3

When Peter calls on slaves to submit to harsh treatment (2.18), even beatings (2.20), is he endorsing slavery? Is he at least suggesting that we should embrace harsh treatment even when we can avoid it?

When we look at 1 Peter's sections addressed to slaves (2.18–25) and wives (3.1–6), we should consider what setting Peter was addressing. He was not addressing a setting of voluntary employees who could simply resign from work if they were being mistreated. He was not addressing women who might readily find different husbands who did not expect unilateral submission.

Peter's advice to both slaves and wives belongs to his larger section of what we have already called household codes, which ancients in turn often discussed in the context of civic management (2.13–3.12). Ancient writers often used such codes to express conventional expectations. For the sake of honouring the Lord (2.12–13), Peter urges compliance when possible with 'every human institution' (2.13). This exhortation does not endorse all these human institutions, such as slavery (2.18–25), empire (2.13, 18) or wives calling their husbands 'lord' (3.6), as universal and eternal. It calls on those in these settings to make the best of their circumstances.

Unless they earned enough money on the side to buy their freedom, slaves did not have much say concerning their slave status. Slaveholders often did eventually free slaves (though sometimes to preclude having to support them in their old age). A minority of slaves in the Roman Empire achieved status and even wealth. But the legal authority to emancipate slaves lay solely with the slaveholders. Peter thus provides advice for how to bear up under a difficult situation that his addressees could not control, not how to resist such a situation. This is the same approach taken by many ancient moral teachers, such as Stoic philosophers, who focused on what is in our power to control, rather than on what is not.

His comments to wives follow along a similar line. (Remember that first word in Greek in 3.1, translated as 'in the same way', explicitly linking the case of wives in 3.1–6 with the case of slaves in 2.18–25.) Addressing wives married to non-believing husbands (3.1), Peter urges them to win over their husbands by gentle and pure behaviour. Illustrating such behaviour, he uses the example of matriarchs such as Sarah who, functioning within the conventional expectations of her culture, obeyed Abraham. Sarah, fitting the convention, calls her husband 'my lord' (Gen. 18.12, though it is not always translated this way from Hebrew), just as others could so address various respected figures (Gen. 18.3; 23.6, 11), including fathers (31.35) and brothers (32.4–5, 18; 33.13–14).

Yet just as Sarah may have done what Abraham said, so also Abraham did what Sarah said (Gen. 16.2), once with God's direct backing (21.12)! So why does Peter offer only the example of Sarah? Only Sarah's example is relevant for these wives, because they cannot control what their husbands will do. Although the degree of power varied, in virtually all cultures Peter addressed, husbands governed their wives.

Yet we need not infer from this an endorsement of universal husbandly rule any more than we infer an endorsement of a universal practice of slavery in 1 Peter 2.18–25. Husbands ruling their wives is common through history, and we might expect as much from the effects of the curse (Gen. 3.16). Yet we are not called to enforce the effects of the curse (for example, requiring men to sweat when they work, or proliferating sin and death as much as possible).

Although Peter is mainly addressing those in subordinate positions in society (1 Peter 2.13), and ancient evidence suggests that women probably outnumbered men in the churches, Peter addresses husbands here as well. He summons them to care for and honour their wives (3.7).

In the case of wives, Peter is addressing the norm in his day, not the question of direct physical abuse that he addressed with slaves (2.20). Unlike slaves, wives were not usually objects of beating in the regions that Peter addresses (1.1). Also unlike slaves, wives had options to safely remove themselves from such situations, if they arose; no laws compelled them to stay. Even Judean Pharisees, who normally recognized only the husband's right to divorce, approved of intervening and making an abusive husband grant a divorce, thus freeing his wife to remarry. In other words, Peter is not advising against escaping such abuse for those with the freedom to do it.

Is it ethical to flee abuse? Scripture provides numerous examples. David fled from Saul, and Jesus' family fled to Egypt to escape Herod. Even in cases of persecution for the name of Christ, Jesus allows fleeing (Matt. 10.23), and his disciples normally did so when possible (Acts 14.6).

Let us be careful to use these passages the way they were meant to be used to encourage one another's faith in the face of difficult situations, not to make those difficult situations harder!

1 Peter 3.8–17

[8] Finally, all of you, have unity of spirit, sympathy, love for one another, a tender heart, and a humble mind. [9] Do not repay evil for evil or abuse for abuse; but, on the contrary, repay with a blessing. It is for this that you were called – that you might inherit a blessing. [10] For

'Those who desire life and desire to see good days, let them keep their tongues from evil and their lips from speaking deceit; [11] let them turn away from evil and do good; let them seek peace and pursue it. [12] For the eyes of the Lord are on the righteous, and his ears are open to their prayer. But the face of the Lord is against those who do evil.'

[13] Now who will harm you if you are eager to do what is good? [14] But even if you do suffer for doing what is right, you are blessed. Do not fear what they fear, and do not be intimidated, [15] but in your hearts sanctify Christ as Lord. Always be ready to make your defence to anyone who demands from you an account of the hope that is in you; [16] yet do it with gentleness and reverence. Keep your conscience clear, so that, when you are maligned, those who abuse you for your good conduct in Christ may be put to shame. [17] For it is better to suffer for doing good, if suffering should be God's will, than to suffer for doing evil.

As we turn to the rest of 1 Peter 3, we find that the remainder of the chapter provides the summary, clarification and broader setting for all that we have read since 2.18. This is marked out clearly at the start of 3.8 where Peter writes 'finally', though the word here could also be translated as 'the conclusion', 'the goal', 'the culmination'. Thus, it is worth us pondering this section carefully, and allowing the sense of direction it gives to shape our understanding of the details within 2.18–3.7, since this is Peter's summary.

There are a number of other linguistic markers that point out that this section is part of the overall argument since 2.11. For example, in 2.12 Peter set out the overall purpose of his instructions as to how Christians should live: that the Christians' manner of life will be a response to those who accuse them of doing evil and a witness to their non-believing neighbours such that they may be converted ('glorify God'). In this he uses the word 'manner of life' or 'conduct' (2.12). Peter repeats the same word in 3.1 when addressing the wives – their 'manner of life' or 'conduct' may bring about the conversion of their husbands. And then again in 3.16, our 'conduct' will make those who speak evil of us ashamed. Thus, the underlying logic of 2.11 through to 3.17 starts to emerge. A manner of life is being advocated that will make it hard for the Christian's neighbours to accuse them, and that may indeed bring those neighbours to faith. This pattern of life is determined not by abstract ideas of 'rights', but wisdom in how to live as a minority in danger of persecution, a minority which believes that even the persecutors can be saved by Jesus.

From the start of this culminating section, Peter calls 'all of you' – not just slaves or wives or any particular sector – to have 'unity of spirit', 'sympathy' (which means to suffer together) and 'love for one another'. These are powerful words coming as they do after 2.18–3.7. For that section dealt with different parts of the community in turn and gave different wisdom for slaves, wives (particularly of unbelieving husbands) and for husbands. That section of 1 Peter could, therefore, give a sense of different rules for different people. But here, in the conclusion, Peter asserts strongly that the 'unity' of the community is vital. The logic is that all the believers – slaves, free, wives, husbands, *all* – need to be together in one mind, viewpoint and purpose, recognize each other as sisters and brothers (joint heirs, 3.7) and bear each other's suffering and burdens. Those burdens – the pressures their distinctive Christian 'conduct' will create – will fall differently on different members of the community, hence the different wisdom to different groups. And yet the conclusion to this section mirrors the start: they are, together in Christ, a holy people, a chosen nation. There is a single calling, even if its application may differ depending on their individual place in the alien society of their exile. This sheds further light on 3.1–6, encouraging us to give full weight to 3.1–2, that wives of non-believing husbands are primarily in view. This is not 'rules for a Christian household', but 'how to cope in exile when you are in a weak position' (hence the parallel advice to slaves).

Within 3.8 and the encompassing instructions of this chapter, the call to have 'a tender heart' is a feeble translation. The word actually refers to the guts and we might paraphrase 'you should be gutted for each other'. A similar word is used for Jesus' feelings towards the people being like sheep without a shepherd (Matt. 9.36) and Jesus' compassion for the leper (Mark 1.41). It is important that we recognize the strong emotion and passion with which Peter exhorts the believers to be together, in order to redress our human tendency to focus on the expressions of difference in the preceding verses.

The call to have 'a humble mind' picks up a thread throughout this section and later in the letter where no one is to lord it over another but always be clothed with humility (5.5). We see this call to be humble in 2.11–3.7, where submission to the ruling authorities in that society has been encouraged following the example of Jesus (2.21–24), and also of others such as Sarah (3.6). Many today feel that in their context God calls them to resist aspects of the injustice of the world around them, rather than bolstering their resilience in humbly coping. That may be true, after all God's calling will be different to different people in different situations, but it is still important that we listen carefully to and ponder God's word through Peter to these people. Indeed, as we have seen, Peter's call is not simply to inner resilience (coping), he does have the transformation of the world in view, but this transformation is through people coming to believe ('glorify God', 2.12; 'won over', 3.2) not the overturning of the structures of society.

'Humble' opens the door to what follows, which has strong parallels in Jesus' teaching in the Sermon on the Mount. Fundamentally the calling is to repay evil with a blessing (3.9), a summary of Jesus' words about loving one's enemy in Matthew 5.43–46. The natural human response is to repay evil for evil, insult with insult, to match power with power, but Jesus' way is different. The parallel is particularly clear in 3.14, where Peter writes, 'if you suffer for doing what is right, you are blessed', which sounds very close to Matthew 5.10: 'Blessed are those who are persecuted for righteousness' sake.'

It is right that we note that this is not normal human behaviour. Jesus' words in the Sermon on the Mount are deeply challenging, and so is Peter's similar call a generation later to the 'exiles' – God's chosen ones living scattered in an alien world. Peter therefore gives at least six reasons to live in this countercultural way of repaying evil with a blessing. Two we have already seen.

1 This distinctive manner of life can bring neighbours to faith in Jesus (2.12; 3.2). While it can seem distasteful to see good coming from oppression, and this in no way justifies the oppression, it is certainly true that today and throughout the Church's history from Saul onwards there are many testimonies to exactly this happening and persecutors coming to faith.

2 This approach could lessen the oppression since generally people are not oppressed for blessing others. Read 3.16: 'so that, when you are maligned, those who abuse you for your good conduct in Christ may be put to shame' (compare 2.12: 'though they malign you as evildoers, they may see your honourable deeds'). Peter does recognize that this is not always true (3.13–14: 'who will harm you if you are eager to do what is good? But even if you do suffer for doing what is right …'; compare 2.15, 19–20 and 3.17) but it is still part of his reasoning.

3 Reason 3 is not explicit is this section, but hinted at and important to note for completeness: the example of Jesus, who himself repaid evil with a blessing (as expounded in 2.21–24). We are reminded of this by the references to Christ: 'sanctify Christ as Lord' (3.15), your 'good conduct in Christ' (3.16). Christ is the origin of this distinctive manner of life. If we are Christ's people and sanctify him as Lord, then we are called to copy his challenging example.

4 Then there are the three reasons explicitly given in 3.9–12. 'It is for this that you were called – that you might inherit a blessing' (3.9). The language of calling, inheritance and blessing reminds us both of the opening chapter of this letter and also has echoes of Abraham (Gen. 12.1–3) who was called, responded and received a blessing. For this reason, Abraham is presented by Paul in Romans 4 as the 'father of the gentiles', who inherit blessing because of their faithful response to God. More broadly it draws on the language of blessings and curses in the Old Testament, as found in for example Deuteronomy 29–30 and Psalm 1: following God's distinctive way of life results in blessing.

5 The last two reasons emerge from the quotation of Psalm 34.12–15 in 1 Peter 3.10–12. The whole psalm is appropriate because it speaks of the assurance God's people can have through hardship, because God is on their side (Ps. 34.10: 'The young lions suffer want and hunger, but those who seek the Lord lack no good thing'; 34.19: 'Many are the afflictions of the righteous, but the Lord rescues them from them all').

Peter draws out two threads from this psalm: the command from God to turn from evil and do good and the command to seek and pursue peace. Peter seems to commend this to his readers implying that their own hardship does not exempt them from this command. They are still obliged to seek and pursue peace. 'Turn away from evil' potentially has two meanings. Most simply 'stop doing evil and do good', but also in this context could imply 'turn from the evil they are doing to you, and do good in response'. Overall though this fifth reason is simply that God tells us all, including those who suffer, to do good and seek peace.

6 Finally, there is the assurance that the Lord sees what is happening and is attentive to prayer. Indeed, God is against those who do evil. In effect this is the assurance that God will rescue and bring justice. We do not need to settle the score because God will. This ties in directly with 1 Peter 2.23: Jesus did not retaliate but entrusted himself to the God who will judge justly. It also echoes the words from Morning Prayer in the *Book of Common Prayer*: 'Give peace in our time, O Lord. Because there is none other than fighteth for us, but only thou, O God.'

These last two reasons for having a distinctive Christian manner of life, repaying evil with a blessing, are helpfully further developed in Romans 12.14–21. This passage begins with echoing the words of the Sermon on the Mount: 'Bless those who persecute you; bless and do not curse them. Rejoice with those who rejoice; weep with those who weep' (12.14–15), then speaks of humility (12.16–17), before giving the command 'do not repay anyone evil for evil' (12.17). Paul then expands on the command to 'live peaceably with all' by adding 'if it is possible, as far as it depends on you', which helpfully shapes reason 5. Yes, Peter's readers should pursue peace. However, because they are generally the people in the weaker position in society, they can only do this to a limited degree. They can only do their bit. It is right to aim for peace, but if the oppressors reject this, they should not feel guilty or pursue peace to their own harm. Romans 12.19 then explains: 'Beloved, never avenge yourselves, but leave room for the wrath of God; for it is written, "Vengeance is mine, I will repay, says the Lord"', which coheres with our reason 6. Their manner of life should not include settling of scores because that is God's role and God will do it. Paul's summary in Romans 12.21 would be equally fitting here: 'Do not be overcome by evil, but overcome evil with good.'

Two further ideas emerge in the final verses of this section. First, in 3.14–15: 'Do not fear what they fear, and do not be intimidated, but in your hearts sanctify Christ as Lord.' The word translated 'be intimidated' is the same used in John 14.1 where Jesus says, 'Do not let your heart be troubled. Believe in God, believe also in me.' It is also the word used to describe the disciples when they see Jesus walking on the water (Mark 6.50; Matt. 14.26) to which Jesus responds, 'Take heart; it is I.' Jesus' Lordship is the reason they should not be troubled or frightened. The word 'sanctify' is also found in the Lord's Prayer: 'sanctified be your name, your kingdom come'.

More broadly 3.14–15 draws on Isaiah 8.11–17, which has already been quoted in 1 Peter 2.8, that Jesus is a stumbling block (Isa. 8.14). Here in 1 Peter 3, the letter focuses on God's commands for Isaiah to have a different lifestyle from his neighbours, to 'not fear what it fears, or be in dread', to sanctify the Lord of Hosts, to 'let him be your fear and let him be your dread' and to wait upon the Lord. It is worth noting that in 1 Peter, the Isaiah passage often translated 'sanctify the Lord of Hosts' is rephrased as 'sanctify Christ as Lord' with Jesus standing in the place of God himself. The same technique for pointing to Jesus being 'God for us' is found elsewhere in the New Testament, such as Philippians 2.11 and 1 Corinthians 8.6. The idea that they should 'fear God' and trust in his protection, is echoed in Jesus' words in Matthew 10.28–29 but also reminds us of the command of Peter in 2.17 to 'fear God'.

That 3.14 is often translated 'do not fear what they fear' is meaningful in our world, gripped by high levels of anxiety, and in which we recognize that psychologically often those who hate and threaten are doing so because they are fearful themselves. This points to the deep truth in Jesus' sacrificial death expounded just a chapter earlier (2.21–24), Jesus' role as a scapegoat, absorbing evil and not repaying it, bearing sins, produced righteousness and healing for others. This is the high calling of Jesus' followers copying his example: to break the cycle of fear, evil and violence, by repaying evil with a blessing. Freedom from fear, therefore, means that we are no longer shaped by what we fear, the evil powers or our anxiety. This freedom, intimately connected to the truth of Christ's suffering, doesn't help us escape from suffering necessarily, but it does mean that our identity is no longer determined by those powers and we can live according to the hope we have in our knowledge of the Lord of the universe. This hope offers serious encouragement for those, like the community of 1 Peter, in difficult times.

Finally in this section, we come to 3.15–16: 'always be ready to make your defence to anyone who demands from you an account of the hope that is in you; yet do it with gentleness and reverence'. Often this verse is twisted by the weight being put on the final words, as if Peter was saying 'you must ensure your evangelism is done more gently', but that is only to excuse our timidity. The weight in the sentence falls on 'ready', 'always' and 'to anyone'. Yes, there is the wisdom that this should be done gently and respectfully: this is sensible given their weak and oppressed position in society, and also follows from the commands to be humble and pursue peace. Nevertheless their calling is to be a blessing to others, to sanctify Jesus, not to be frightened into silence, and indeed the aim of their manner of life is that others might be won over to glorify God.

Underlying this is a logic for evangelism that we find elsewhere in the New Testament but that is often overlooked. Peter's readers are urged to live in a distinctive manner and then to be ready to answer the questions about their faith that emerge: the manner of life provokes the questions, but the questions then need to be answered. Too often we fail at one or other of these challenges: either we don't have a distinctive and attractive enough conduct to provoke any questions, or we do but are unwilling when asked to point people to Jesus being the source of our life. Neither actions nor words alone are sufficient. But nor is it as simple as saying we need both. Peter's vision appears to be that the distinctive manner of life (the actions) needs to come first and generate genuine interest and questions, then the gentle explanation of a living hope in Jesus can be given. We see this played out on the day of Pentecost (Acts 2.1–41) when the actions of the Jesus' disciples as they receive the Spirit causes people to question 'What does this mean?', to which Peter was able to give an answer, speaking of Jesus and God's offer of salvation. That is the approach to adopt according to this letter, even though Peter himself knew that some would also scoff (Acts 2.13), stumble (1 Peter 2.8) and oppress (3.14, suffering for doing what is right; 3.16 slandered for their good manner of life).

The themes from this section continue in what follows (3.18–22). In this final section, Peter speaks again of the example of Jesus, highlighting that he suffered unjustly, and God used this to bring blessing to others, and indeed to them, speaking of the need both for patience and for confidence. Further echoes of this call and this pattern of life continue throughout 1 Peter. For example, 1 Peter 5.1–11 begins with some focused teaching towards 'elders' and then 'younger people' (as here we have encountered words to slaves and wives) which then leads to instruction to 'everyone' focused around humility, the reality that suffering will come, and the need to trust in God who will not let them down.

---

1 Peter 3.18–22

[18] For Christ also suffered for sins once for all, the righteous for the unrighteous, in order to bring you to God. He was put to death in the flesh, but made alive in the spirit, [19] in which also he went and made a proclamation to the spirits in prison, [20] who in former times did not obey, when God waited patiently in the days of Noah, during the building of the ark, in which a few, that is, eight people, were saved through water. [21] And baptism, which this prefigured, now saves you – not as a removal of dirt from the body, but as an appeal to God for a good conscience, through the resurrection of Jesus Christ, [22] who has gone into heaven and is at the right hand of God, with angels, authorities, and powers made subject to him.

These final five verses bring 1 Peter 3 to a close. This is a chapter that has focused on the response the gospel demands and the central place that the actions of Christ himself take, in his life and in his suffering, inseparable from what is demanded of those who follow him. This final section builds on the actions of Christ that enable the community of 1 Peter to be 'free people' and 'God's own people', emphasizing what God in Christ has done and will continue to do for the people of God and how the Church's unity and union with Christ is sealed though baptism.

It is suggested in 3.18 that the suffering and vulnerability of the Church during its time of exile (1.17) in the world is a sign and result of its participation in Christ. This affirmation seeks to uphold those who suffer for doing what is right (3.13–17). It also underlines how the suffering of Christ is the model for the life of the believer. The faithful follower of Jesus is to do what is right, regardless of the fact that this may result in one's own suffering. This message is bolstered by an emphasis on the cosmic scope of Christ's action. For the one who innocently suffers the cross is nevertheless ruler and Lord of the world. Although put to death, he was 'made alive in the spirit' (3.18).

This theme runs alongside the affirmation that the righteous suffering of Christ is undertaken for the unrighteous. This not only once again reminds Peter's community that its present difficulties are trivial compared to the trials undertaken by Christ on its behalf, it also reminds the Church that Christ is the one who removes sin and enables godly behaviour.

Initially, 3.19–21 might strike the reader as an abrupt shift in tone and focus. Indeed, the reference to Christ proclaiming 'to the spirits in prison' baffled Martin Luther, who dismissed the passage as a strange text. In certain regions of the world, there is need for caution here, given that some readers might associate these 'spirits' with their non-Christian ancestors and relations who have passed from this life. Is this text making certain statements about the fate of such people?

Understanding these verses is complicated by the obscure nature of the text in Greek. Peter suggests that 'in the spirit', Christ 'also' 'went'. The main issue here is whether this movement of Christ refers to his descending or ascending (into hell, or the ascension into heaven). The text itself is terribly unclear.

Excursus: Who or What are 'the spirits in prison'?

John Elliott identifies four main interpretations of 3.19–21 among the enormous amount of existing commentary.

The first interpretation suggests that Christ descended to the realm of the dead prior to his resurrection to announce a message to dead human beings ('spirits'). Those who advocate this view debate whether this audience consists of the generation of Noah and its potential conversion, or only those of that generation who converted prior to death, or whether this 'proclamation' was not an offer of conversion but only one of condemnation to Noah's unbelieving contemporaries.

A second approach suggests that Christ, in his pre-existent nature, preached repentance to Noah's contemporaries during their lifetime.

A third view suggests a variant of the second, arguing that Christ descended to the realm of the dead to announce salvation to those of Noah's generation who repented prior to their death.

A fourth interpretation links 1 Peter 3.19–20 to a tradition of the flood story that is found in 1 Enoch. In this Jewish text, the events that lead to the flood are associated with evil spirits who lead God's people into corruption. Interpretations of 3.19–20 that see a link to 1 Enoch thus understand the 'spirits in prison' to be sinful angelic spirits, to whom Christ announces their condemnation.

Elliott, along with interpreters like Douglas Harink and Paul Achtemeier, develop this fourth approach to 3.19–20 on the basis that they think it

> provides the clearest way to make sense of the
> passage, as well as for the way in which it coincides
> with the discussion of baptism that follows in 3.21.

To elaborate on the reading of 3.19–20 developed in
the excursus above and to try to bring some clarity
to what Peter means, scholars interpret the meaning
of 'in the spirit' and 'also' as referring to events after
Christ's resurrection when he was 'made alive' after
being 'put to death' (3.18). The significance of this
interpretation is that the events described in 3.19
are understood as acts of the risen Christ. After
Christ's death, through the resurrection, he is 'made
alive in the spirit' and then offers his proclamation
to the 'spirits in prison'. Christ's announcement is
thus not offered to dead human beings in some dark
underworld, but rather to spiritual powers who are
in rebellion against God and who cause evil in the
world.

This understanding of the text avoids becoming
entangled in the concerns of those who, in some
contexts, might presume that the 'spirits in prison'
refer to their ancestors. Furthermore, this way of
regarding the difficult passage connects neatly and
logically to what follows about baptism in 3.21–22.
Peter describes the story of the flood from Genesis
in 3.20 as a prefigured anticipation of the waters
of baptism (3.21). The ark of salvation for the

'eight people ... saved through water' is a sign of the messianic community of the Church. As such the act of baptism that 'now saves you' is an act that defies the lord-less powers who are in rebellion against Christ.

Another consideration that encourages this interpretation is the way in which it emboldens the reader to stay focused on his or her own calling and response to Christ. Instead of distracting the reader to speculate on the external fate of Noah's generation, 1 Peter clarifies that Christ's proclamation is directed against active spiritual powers rather than dead human beings. Thus, Peter encourages believers to understand their baptism as an act of resistance against the powers of evil and encourages them to give thanks for God's saving work in the face of trial.

The main message to be heard in this section is thus that Christ has delivered those living as 'aliens and exiles' from slavery to the powers of evil even as they continue to live in separation or diaspora from the fullness of God's kingdom. Despite any appearance to the contrary, the forces of death and destruction do not have the last word or ultimate authority over this world or the believer, for Christ rules 'at the right hand of God, with angels, authorities, and powers made subject to him' (3.22). The text suggests that through baptism as an ultimate act of salvation, the Church – as the body of Christ and the ark of God – receives its free and joyful existence from the resurrected Christ.

Thus, 3.15–16 serves as a hinge for this chapter and for the whole of the letter as those who follow Christ are told to be ready to make a testimony for the hope that is in them, even in the midst of great suffering. This is not dreary work but is a testimony of joy in the resurrected victory of Christ, who offers a living hope, and to whom in the end, all powers submit. In resurrection life, Jesus preaches even to the spirits in prison and is always victor, so that those who live under conditions they cannot control – illness, pain, unjust regimes, unjust authority – all live as children of this Lord who in his suffering was redeeming the world and in his victory is Lord and judge of this world. The central affirmation in this chapter, as in the letter as a whole, is that we are not left comfortless but live in a world where Christ is Lord. So while it may look to us – in the midst of what are sometimes difficult and even unbearable situations for us – that others are in control of this world, in virtue of the resurrection of Christ, there is only one true judge and Lord and we are the 'living stones' of his house and his own holy people.

Questions for reflection

1 1 Peter gives clear instruction to those who are
   living under human institutions, those who are
   enslaved, and to wives and husbands in 2.13–3.7.
   Wives and slaves are explicitly compared.

   • Why are we more confident in condemning
     slavery than patriarchy in our world?

   • How might this section of 1 Peter speak in our
     contemporary context?

   • What might hope look like if Jesus is Lord and
     not the emperor, master, or husband?

   • What do we take from this section of 1 Peter for
     women and men in our world who are trafficked
     as domestic workers or sex slaves?

   • What do we take from this section of 1 Peter for
     wives in our world who are repeatedly abused
     by their husbands?

   • How do we account for the history of the Angli-
     can Church in South Africa under apartheid,
     for example, when some like Desmond Tutu
     rejected the compliant resilience of 1 Peter
     and argued for overt resistance, and other
     Anglicans counselled conformity to apartheid
     authority, citing 1 Peter?

   • What is the difference between resistance and
     resilience when you feel you are invisible or
     persecuted? According to 1 Peter, can you judge

the right response to oppression for someone in a different situation from you?

2 1 Peter asks Christians to always be ready to make a defence of the hope that is in you to anyone who demands an account from you.

- How do you live in a way that your life provokes questions about hope?
- Why does this verse suggest that we must wait to be asked?
- How is suffering, especially Jesus' suffering, a source of hope?
- Can you give an account of the hope that is in you?

3 1 Peter speaks of baptism as an act of salvation and a sign that all who are baptized are subject to Christ.

- How does baptism kindle hope?
- What does it mean for all to be subject to Christ?

4

Suffering in Christ
(1 Peter 4)

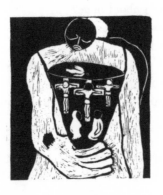

'Crucifixion' (1977), Lindiwe Mvemve.

'Crucifixion': the reality that the Christian community shares in the sufferings of Christ is a theme that runs throughout 1 Peter. This painting depicts the cup of suffering Christ accepts, except that the cup is held by God the Father and, magnified in size, it contains the scene of the crucifixion of God's Son. Here, we see the sadness and suffering that this cup brings, depicting Christ's death between two criminals, his alienation and abandonment by all except the beloved disciple and his mother (John 19.26), and the Spirit of consolation hovering nearby, a symbol of living hope. This hope, as found in 1 Peter, is implied in the largeness of the cup through which God takes into God's very self all human suffering in order to redeem it.

Lindiwe Mvemve, South African artist, from the HKV-Museum Sankt Augustin collection, used by permission. See www.imb. org/2017/04/12/journey-cross-artists-visualize-christs-passion-part-2/.

In the first chapter, we encountered suffering as one of the central themes of 1 Peter. The recipients of this letter are suffering, Christ's suffering and exaltation are the example for all who suffer (2.18–25) and Christians are called to follow Christ and to know Christ's joy in the midst of suffering (3.18–22). Now, in chapter 4, Peter gets into the heart of what he means by suffering, unpacking what suffering means for his community.

Suffering has been raised in every chapter before this and is mentioned more times in 1 Peter than in any other New Testament text. We have to remember 1 Peter's context as a letter written to a small group of Christians who are a minority in their culture and who live in an empire that is hostile to them, fearful of their beliefs, worship other gods and view Christians with suspicion. Within this context, Peter describes suffering in a few ways, beginning with what it is and what it is not. He is not speaking about suffering because a person is evil. He is speaking only about suffering for the name of Christ.

It is clear from 1 Peter 4, therefore, that not all suffering is redemptive. Even though Christians are called to imitate Christ in his suffering, suffering is different in different situations. What is essential, however, and what ties together all of the suffering of which Peter speaks is the connection of suffering to Christ and to being Christian. Suffering for being Christian, for being called 'Christian', is a central part of 1 Peter 4, which is ultimately framed by the promise that those who suffer 'for the name of Christ' will share in the glory of God, blessed by the Spirit (4.14). And even though Peter is writing about something that is very real and painful for his community, he nevertheless frames it with hope, reminding his hearers that suffering does not have the final word.

The chapter is relevant not only for Peter's time and context, but for many Christians around the world today. While some Christians have the privilege of following Christ without the threat of suffering associated with his name, in many parts of the world being Christian results in great suffering, including the threat of death, imprisonment and limitations on identity. And so, this profoundly relevant text reminds us that as Christians who are part of one holy nation (2.9), we are to be mindful of and share in one another's sufferings.

How precisely we do this is the other crucial

focus of 1 Peter 4, which picks up on themes already encountered in the letter: mutual love, prayer and discipline. To this, Peter introduces a new behaviour to which his community is called: hospitality without grumbling (4.9). This theme of hospitality, a term that literally means 'love of the stranger', is an essential response to following Christ, to imitating Christ. For 1 Peter, hospitality is a central element of the Christian calling. Remembering that the community of 1 Peter are 'aliens and exiles', the call of a people displaced in the world to love the stranger and embody suffering is radical. These central themes – suffering and hospitality – are the focus from the very start of chapter 4.

1 Peter 4.1–6

[1] Since therefore Christ suffered in the flesh, arm yourselves also with the same intention (for whoever has suffered in the flesh has finished with sin), [2] so as to live for the rest of your earthly life no longer by human desires but by the will of God. [3] You have already spent enough time in doing what the Gentiles like to do, living in licentiousness, passions, drunkenness, revels, carousing, and lawless idolatry. [4] They are surprised that you no longer join them in the same excesses of dissipation, and so they blaspheme. [5] But they will have to give an account to him who stands ready to judge the living and the dead.

> 6 For this is the reason the gospel was proclaimed even to the dead, so that, though they had been judged in the flesh as everyone is judged, they might live in the spirit as God does.

1 Peter 4 begins with a foundational premise: 'Christ suffered in the flesh'. From the very first sentence of this chapter, suffering is front and centre, but with an important caveat. Peter is not writing about any suffering; he is writing about the suffering of Jesus Christ. Just as 'Christ suffered in the flesh' so Peter's community is 'also with the same intention' to suffer. Peter is not glorifying suffering but speaks only of suffering for Christ's glory.

That 'Christ suffered in the flesh' refers especially to Christ's death, a connection made clear from Peter's description of Jesus in the previous chapter (see 3.18). However, and significantly, Peter isn't calling his community to death and martyrdom. 'Christ's sufferings' certainly include his passion and death on the cross, but they may well be broader. Throughout his ministry, Jesus experienced hostility, rejection by his closest associates, economic vulnerability, as well as physical pain. Christ's sufferings, therefore, embrace more than the suffering of those who are facing the penalty of death. Christ's sufferings include all who are mocked, rejected, vulnerable and in pain because of their faith. Peter encourages his community in their suffering by directly addressing and acknowledging that their suffering is real and offering them a perspective to find encouragement, even joy, in the midst of their trials. And that perspective is simple: Christ also suffered.

Peter is clear that suffering is not something that his community endures passively, but since Christ suffered, they are to 'arm' themselves with this same 'way of thinking' (4.1). The language of 'arming' may well draw on a military image, like Paul's images of putting on spiritual armour (see Eph. 6.11–16). However, despite the military metaphor this attitude is fundamentally non-violent, not departing from the stance found throughout this letter. Like Christ, they should refuse to return abuse with abuse (2.23). What they arm themselves with are not physical weapons, but the insight that they are sharing in the sufferings of Christ (4.13).

Suffering should not surprise Christ's followers who know the story of Christ's suffering and the stories of the sufferings endured by God's people Israel. That the community suffers should not come as a shock, 'as though something strange were happening to you' (4.12). Suffering, rather than material blessings, is the default position of those God loves. As we know and will read explicitly in this chapter, the audience of 1 Peter is experiencing 'a fiery ordeal' (4.12). This could refer to official Roman persecution, but likely also refers to hostility and suspicion from non-Christian neighbours, occasionally erupting into violence. Such suffering is a sharing or communion in the sufferings of Christ (4.13).

Addressing Christians with little power Peter, in a not unexpected move, locates their unjust sufferings in the context of the Christian hope. Christ's glory is still to be revealed (4.13), and the glory of that end is a beacon towards which his community is called to orient their lives. Suffering will ultimately be overcome. Nevertheless, this hope and future orientation in the *then* doesn't mean that Christians are not called to action *now*. That suffering for faith will be overcome doesn't suggest not doing good. Here we remember the repeated call to do good when Peter addressed community members suffering in various ways in 2.18–3.7.

Thus, 4.2 finishes the first sentence with the understanding that because Christ suffered, there are consequences for the way the community must live. These consequences concern not only a call to embrace the same intention as Christ, even though only Christ can defeat sin once for all, but also encourages Christians to live by the will of God and not human desires. The term for 'desires' (or passions) also appears in 1.14 and 2.11, and is illustrated in concrete examples in 4.3. These desires characterize the believers' pre-Christian past (1.14) and the worldly existence to which they no longer belong (2.11). Although some philosophers applied the language of passions to any emotion, Jewish and Christian sources usually use this language only for illicit passions (for example, desiring one's spouse is not sinful, but desiring someone else's is).

As such, the list in 4.3 includes passions, but these are placed alongside a number of other behaviours which in some ancient contexts are associated with male Gentiles. As we know, Peter addresses primarily Gentiles who have become a new people in Christ (2.9), and thus he is clear that they should no longer live like Gentiles and partake in the forms of immorality illustrated here. Peter has already given us a list of vices at the start of chapter 2 concerning how we live (or are not to live!) in community (malice, guile, insincerity, envy, slander) and now expands it to include a number of specific actions. Ancient writers commonly listed vices, which mirror many of those found in 1 Peter 4 involving sexual immorality, drunkenness, and venerating idols. It's worth noting that the issue with drunkenness is not drinking or drunken parties, but drunkenness that entails loss or reduction of self-control.

Not behaving in these ways, however, also has consequences. Because non-believers will be 'surprised' by the new and different lifestyle of the believer (4.4), believers who give up these vices are noticed by those around them and become rather exposed and vulnerable. That they no longer participate with others in these behaviours will lead to social suffering. Therefore, by contrast, believers should *not* be 'surprised' (the same Greek word; 4.12) by their sufferings because Christ's suffering also included being marginalized and mocked (see 4.14 and Mark 15.27–32; Rom. 15:3). The word 'blaspheme' in 4.4 follows along these lines and simply means to 'speak against'.

Peter then moves to a statement of judgement against those who blaspheme, for they will have to give an account to the one who judges justly. This ties in directly with 1 Peter 2.12 and 2.23: Jesus did not retaliate but entrusted himself to the God who will judge justly. Once again in 4.5, we have the suggestion of eschatological or end-time vindication for God's servants: those who are surprised by the believers' good actions and blaspheme them for their changed behaviour will be judged. This can echo the theme of reversal in the Gospels, as also in 5.6: those who dishonour God's servants now will someday have to answer to God. That God will judge the living and the dead (as also in Acts 10.42; 2 Tim. 4.1; Rom. 14.9) reminds us that the vindication will come, whether before or after death. Moreover, that God will judge the living and the dead (4.5) essentially means everyone. Judgement thus isn't simply divine retribution against those who oppress or those who live according to certain vices; all stand under God's judgement.

While Peter tells his community not to be surprised by their suffering, it is a surprise to some who read this text that the good news (as in Chapter 2: the gospel) was preached to the dead. The result of this proclamation is that even though some were judged by humans as unworthy, they may live. Interpreters divide as to the sense of what Peter means in 4.6. Traditionally, many believed that the point was that Jesus preached to the dead in Hades. A majority of scholars today, however, understand the verse as referring to the gospel being preached to those who are *now* dead, but were alive when the gospel was preached to them (see also 1.25). On this latter interpretation, those who have been accused by human judges, those who have been judged unjustly by human judges ('in the flesh'), will ultimately be vindicated and raised from the dead 'in the spirit' (4.6), because they were righteous and God is the one who will judge ultimately.

These two interpretations of 4.6 correspond to the various major views that we encountered in the interpretation of 3.18–22 concerning the 'spirits in prison'. As we found in Chapter 3, many scholars believed that the spirits in prison in 3.19 were the deceased to whom Christ preached in Hades. Others believed that Christ preached through Noah to those in Noah's day while they were still alive. A majority of modern scholars find more corres-pondences with Jewish traditions about Enoch that were widespread in Peter's era where those being preached to were fallen angels. On this view, Christ's exaltation over the angelic powers in 3.22 includes his proclamation of victory over them: all 'angels, authorities, and powers' are 'made subject' to Christ. 4.6 draws on the preceding context even if those receiving the gospel proclamation are not angels or spirits. Jesus was executed in the flesh but raised by God's Spirit (3.18), and thus believers may be punished in the flesh (physically), but will be raised by God's Spirit (see also Rom 1.4; 8.10–11). Read in this way, the central encouragement to the community of 1 Peter is emphasized: in their suffering for bearing the name of Christ, they join Jesus in his sufferings in the flesh and are promised a share in his glorification, raised by God's Spirit. To suffer for Christ is to be joined to the resurrected Lord.

1 Peter 4.7–11

[7] The end of all things is near; therefore be serious and discipline yourselves for the sake of your prayers. [8] Above all, maintain constant love for one another, for love covers a multitude of sins. [9] Be hospitable to one another without complaining. [10] Like good stewards of the manifold grace of God, serve one another with whatever gift each of you has received. [11] Whoever speaks must do so as one speaking the very words of God; whoever serves must do so with the strength that God supplies, so that God may be glorified in all things through Jesus Christ. To him belong the glory and the power for ever and ever. Amen.

The pressure is maintained in 4.7 for those who are called to a new way of living, for the end is near and therefore they must maintain a sense of seriousness and discipline. This is more than simple scare-mongering that Jesus is coming and judgement is to be feared. Rather, in the context of suffering, the nearness of 'the end' can encourage those longing for future vindication (4.5–6; see also 1.4–5, 7, 9; 5.4, 6, 10). The term for 'end' here is used elsewhere in 1 Peter to apply to the 'outcome' of faith in 1.9, namely, ultimate salvation, and also in 4.17 to describe the outcome of judgement for those who disobey the gospel.

Just as ancient writers in general often connected the language of being 'disciplined' or sober with not being caught unexpectedly, early Christians often associated it with being ready for Christ's return (for example, 1 Thess. 5.6–7). This association probably goes back to Jesus' own teaching (Matt. 24.42–51; Mark 13.23, 33–37; Luke 21.36). This warning appears three times in 1 Peter (1.13; 5.8; and here). It might be difficult for us to share the perspective that the 'end of all things is near' as 2,000 years later we know the end has not yet come. And yet here we can embrace a sense of what it means to long for an end to suffering, and for suffering to be exchanged for God's blessing and glory.

So far in this chapter, the focus has been primarily on what believers are not to do, with a list of behaviours they are to leave behind (4.3), and now

with the exhortation to be serious and disciplined,
Peter builds on how they are called to live since
'Christ suffered in the flesh'. Beginning with 4.8,
Peter offers clear reminders of familiar themes and
conduct required of his community, beginning with
'constant love for one another'. Certainly ancient
Jewish teachers valued love, but early Christianity
was a movement in which love was consistently and
pervasively the chief virtue. And this love isn't just
for the sake of the individual or for salvation; the
purpose of love here is inclusion and unity 'for love
covers a multitude of sins' (see also Prov. 10.12;
James 5.20). With the theme of God's judgement
fresh on the readers' minds, when faced with sin
and the behaviour of the Gentiles, the Christian
community is not called to judge these sins or this
behaviour but to love. And this is a love rooted
not in judgement but in the forgiveness and love of
God. Such language echoes the call in the opening
chapter of this letter to 'have genuine mutual love,
love one another deeply from the heart' (1.22). This
is the kind of love that will enable the Christian
community to avoid the malice, slander, resentment
and strife that can result if they are not prepared to
forgive (Horrell 2008, pp. 81–2).

But love isn't the only action that believers are
called to engage in, for 4.9 introduces another
essential element of communal life: hospitality
without grumbling. It's a comment that can make
us smile as it implies that even this early Christian

community struggled with complaining hosts and difficult guests from time to time. 'Hospitality' here is a Greek term that means 'love for strangers' (in contrast to xenophobia – fear of strangers), which is a fascinating call for those who are 'aliens and exiles'. Showing kindness to strangers in antiquity could be expressed in something as little as providing a cup of cold water, if that was all that one had. Because inns were dangerous, Jewish homeowners often offered a place to stay for other Jewish people who were passing through; this hospitality could even extend for two or three weeks. The *Didache*, another early Christian source, shows how Christians welcomed travelling ministers, although also speaks about how they had to be discerning and guard against abuses.

That believers should show hospitality to one another fits the image of believers as 'resident aliens' in a world to which they no longer belong (1.1; 2.11). We remember that they are not migrants, displaced from their historic homes so to speak, but they became outsiders when they converted. And here, as in chapter 2, there are behavioural consequences for being 'aliens and exiles'. Because they share the same alienation from the world, they must offer a welcoming home for one another. Just as love must be sincere, without hypocrisy (1.22), so hospitality must be without grumbling. 'Complaining' or 'murmuring' here is the same language used to describe Israel's complaining against God in the wilderness (1 Cor. 10.10).

And yet, just as those who are aliens and exiles have been given status as God's chosen people, so hospitality changes the status of all those involved in the act. The person receiving hospitality, the person who is offered love and welcome, is no longer a stranger. Just as aliens and exiles were once not a people and now are God's people (2.10), so the person receiving hospitality was once a stranger and now is no longer. But curiously, the status of the one offering the hospitality is also changed in the act, for by loving one who is a stranger and vulnerable, they too are made vulnerable. Hospitality involves risk. There is a reason that some of the greatest hostility Jesus faced was when he restored others and shared a meal with them, when he offered and received hospitality.

Excursus: Hospitality

The First Letter of Peter presupposes that Christians will show hospitality to one another (4:9). The Greek word for hospitality, *philoxenos*, literally means 'love of the stranger' or 'love of the foreigner'. Hospitality in the ancient world was considered a virtuous act, whereby a household might entertain the gods, or visiting angels (Gen. 18.1–15; see also Heb. 13.2). For the traveller, it was much safer than staying in inns, many of which had a poor reputation, or sleeping outside along the road. For the host who was poor, however, hospitality could be costly: sharing already meagre resources such as food, water and a place to sleep.

Both Jews and Christians prized hospitality, which offered a network of fellow believers and ensured a welcome place of refuge. This love of strangers has particular poignancy in 1 Peter, addressed to Christians who have become 'aliens and exiles' for their commitment to Christ (2.11). In showing hospitality, strangers welcome strangers, foreigners show love to foreigners, recognizing their common kinship in Christ. In a world that is often fearful of strangers, 1 Peter speaks of strangers whom God has made friends.

Peter's expectations of hospitality are tempered by reality as he calls the community to offer hospitality 'with whatever gift each of you has received' (4.10). They are, of course, to be good stewards of God's grace, which we remember from elsewhere in this letter is a gift from God. The Greek term translated 'gift' here was still rare in this period, so it is probably no coincidence that Paul uses the term in a similar way (see 1 Cor. 12.4). Peter probably refers to the same idea: God has graced each of us with different gifts and therefore we can use these to serve one another. And from these gifts, which in this letter have been described as holiness, grace and salvation, the Christian is to 'love the stranger' and 'serve one another'.

The language of 'steward' in 4.10 is literally 'household manager' (see also Luke 12.42–48). While the person in such a position could be a slave or a free person, they held high status within a wealthy household, and this image fits with the image of the Church as a house or household elsewhere in 1 Peter (2.5; 4.17). Peter's community are called to be good stewards, active stewards, sharing the gifts they have received from God and welcoming all into the spiritual house, made up of living stones. Peter makes clear in what follows, however, that none of this is by one's own strength. Christ and the grace of God remain absolutely central to all action.

Peter elaborates this notion of gifts in 4.11, although he offers only two sorts of examples: speaking and serving. One gift entails speaking 'the very words of God', for which the term here is 'oracles of God', an expression that often refers to prophetic utterances. This may refer to the spiritual gift of prophecy, which Paul sometimes mentions towards the beginning of his lists of spiritual gifts (Rom. 12.6; 1 Cor. 12.28). Alternatively, it may refer to all sorts of speaking (including teaching), especially when we think back to Peter's play on the word 'word' in 1 Peter 3.7, suggesting that we should depend on God's grace for any speaking, as we would if we were prophesying. Likewise, relying on God's strength to serve is also associated with hospitality (see also Rom. 12.7, although there the NRSV translates the related term as 'ministering'). In this ministry of hospitality, we must depend on God's strength. By acknowledging our dependence on God, we credit God for what he accomplishes through us, bringing him honour and glory 'through Jesus Christ'. This goal of God being glorified through Christ is one we have encountered throughout this letter as the goal of Christian conduct and the basis for how Peter's community is to respond in difficult situations.

When we stand back from the call to love and hospitality in this section on suffering, we notice that these actions to which the Christian community of 1 Peter is called are about drawing people together. All people in the community are challenged to use their gifts for the common good (Horrell 1998, p. 83). We live in a diverse world that faces many challenges and suffering can be something that either pulls us inward or pulls us apart, making us fearful or anxious, and rightly so. But this text calls all, especially those who might be suffering less, to move towards those who are suffering and to support them with genuine love and hospitality.

1 Peter 4.12–19

[12] Beloved, do not be surprised at the fiery ordeal that is taking place among you to test you, as though something strange were happening to you. [13] But rejoice in so far as you are sharing Christ's sufferings, so that you may also be glad and shout for joy when his glory is revealed. [14] If you are reviled for the name of Christ, you are blessed, because the spirit of glory, which is the Spirit of God, is resting on you. [15] But let none of you suffer as a murderer, a thief, a criminal, or even as a mischief-maker. [16] Yet if any of you suffers as a Christian, do not consider it a disgrace, but glorify God because you bear this name. [17] For the time has come for judgement to begin with the household of God; if it begins with us, what will be the end for those who do not obey the gospel of God? [18] And 'If it is hard for the righteous to be saved, what will become of the ungodly and the sinners?' [19] Therefore, let those suffering in accordance with God's will entrust themselves to a faithful Creator, while continuing to do good.

This section returns once again to the central concern of 1 Peter to encourage a community who are suffering and facing persecution. It begins by repeating an exhortation concerning 'surprise', the second of only three instances of this word in the

New Testament outside Acts (the other instance being in Heb. 13.2). Earlier the surprise was on the side of those who blaspheme, the world so to speak. Now the surprised ones are the Christian community, except that they are told that they should not be 'surprised'. Because they are aliens or strangers within the world (1.1; 2.13), they should not count it as 'alien' or 'strange' when they face testing in this world. The term translated 'surprised' can also mean 'entertain as a guest', and the related term translated 'strange' can mean a 'stranger' or foreigner. Thus, the term can also mean, 'show hospitality to strangers', like a related expression in 4.9, but here the believers are the strangers, from whom the world is estranged.

Excursus: Strangers

Stranger language echoes throughout this chapter. Gentile neighbours 'find it strange' that believers refrain from the excesses of their former life (4.4). Believers are not to 'find it strange' when they experience suffering, as if that were something 'strange' or 'foreign' (4.12). They are to show hospitality or 'love of stranger' without grumbling (4.9). What for the outsider is a sign of strangeness, for Christians has become a mark of familiarity. In Christ, they are strangers no more. Because this is the curious consequence of hospitality: when a stranger is shown hospitality, they are no longer a stranger. A status change happens with hospitality. The nameless stranger has a name; the destabilized sojourner has stability.

The image of a 'fiery ordeal' in 4.12 recalls 1.7, in which believers' faith is tested by fire. This could relate to the emperor Nero's burning of Christians as torches (a persecution in which we have reason to believe that Peter himself died). Nevertheless, it was also an image very familiar from the Old Testament (Job 23.10; Ps. 66.10; Prov. 17.3; 27.21; Isa. 48.10; Ezek. 22.18, 20, 22; Dan. 11.35; 12.10; Zech. 13.9; Mal. 3.2). The outcome of such testing, for those who persevere, is honour for Christ (1 Peter 1.7) and full vindication (4.5–7).

Once again, as soon as Peter turns to suffering described by the 'fiery ordeal' and testing, the person of Christ is close at hand. For no sufferings, no testing or fiery trials for the faith are undertaken separate from Christ's own suffering. In 4.13, Peter gives reasons to take courage when his community is persecuted, tested, or mocked for Christ. Those whose sufferings share in Christ's sufferings can rejoice, 'be glad and shout for joy', because they will also share Christ's glory. Far from a surprising situation, suffering for the name of Christ is an occasion for joy as it is a sign that they share in the sufferings of Christ. Rejoicing in the face of suffering for Christ is a common early Christian theme, encountered already at the start of this letter (1 Peter 1.6–8; see also Acts 5.41; Rom. 5; 2 Cor. 1.5–7; James 1). It presumably reflects Jesus' teaching, in which his followers are blessed when they are mocked (Matt. 5.11–12; Luke 6.22–23). There is a challenge in this part of the letter for all who call themselves Christian to rejoice, even in the midst of suffering, naming the reality emphasized throughout 1 Peter of the hope one has in Christ and the future glory promised.

This letter is shot through with hints of glory (1.7, 11, 21, 24; 4.11, 13, 14; 5.1, 4, 10) and we find the word 'glory' and 'glorify' in this letter an astonishing 14 times, including here in 4.13 and 14. The underlying Greek term has a range of meaning: 'glory', 'brightness', 'fame' and 'honour'. In the Old Testament, God's glory was God's radiant, powerful presence among God's people, whether in the pillar of fire, the wilderness tabernacle, or the Jerusalem temple. For 1 Peter, God's glorious presence is already experienced now, through the Holy Spirit (4.14). But this is only a foretaste of the glory still to be revealed at Christ's coming (4.13). Present suffering will give way to future glory, as it has already for the suffering Christ whom God raised from the dead (1.11, 21). Therefore, one of the motives for doing good and persevering in the midst of suffering is that Peter's community has a living hope, which is intimately connected to future vindication and to glory.

Thus in 4.14, the blessing of God – the promised inheritance found in 1 Peter 3.9 – is directly connected to the 'spirit of glory' 'resting on you'. Believers are blessed not only because they suffer in fellowship with Christ (4.13), awaiting his glory that will be revealed, but also because they already experience the Spirit that brings glory, the Spirit of God (4.14). The Spirit provides a foretaste of future glory (Rom. 8.23; 1 Cor. 2.9–10; 2 Cor. 1.22; 5.5; Gal. 5.5; Eph. 1.13–14; Heb. 6.4–5) and an assurance of God's presence in the here and now of suffering. That they are reviled for bearing the name of Christ, language similar to the Beatitudes in Matthew and Luke (Matt. 5.11–12; Luke 6.22), assures them that they are blessed and the Spirit of God is 'resting on you'.

And yet Peter clarifies once again that the suffering of which he speaks is not just any suffering (see also 2.19–20; 3.17). Suffering as a criminal or even a 'mischief-maker' was not the kind of suffering Peter envisaged. For Peter, not all suffering is redemptive. Of the examples encountered in 4.15, chains, imprisonment, conviction and the like were considered causes of great shame in antiquity; most people did not want to be associated with someone so punished. Of course, this carried over to the embarrassment of some about the cross: the Roman state had executed Jesus – although they could not keep him dead. One should not bring reproach on the name of Christ by suffering for real crimes. But if one suffers as a Christian, this was not genuinely worthy of shame (4.16). Here, Peter takes that which is shameful and reclaims it. Christ, who died a shameful death as a criminal, vindicates and lifts up all through his suffering. The name 'Christian', which was a derogatory name given to those who followed Christ (Acts 11.26), becomes a term of honour and points directly to God.

The word 'Christian' occurs only three times in the New Testament, here in 1 Peter and twice in Acts. We know that outsiders first called believers 'Christians' (Acts 11.26; 26.28), probably as a title of derision. Here (4.16) it might be used as something like a legal charge. Others might ridicule one as a Christian, trying to shame those who are associated with the name of Christ, but this ridicule, this suffering for Jesus' name is, for Peter, an opportunity to honour God. The God who made the shameful cross a throne of victory, the God who makes the unholy holy (1.13–16) will vindicate those who bear Christ's name (4.13). Here, once again, we encounter the language of 'glory' and the call of all to 'glorify God' even in suffering.

When we think about suffering for the name of Christ, this will mean very different things depending on where we are in the world and how we hear this text. Peter is pointing to persecution for one's faith. In some parts of our world, that persecution might take the form of some kind of social pushback. But in other parts of the world, this persecution involves the daily threat of physical violence, oppression, even death. We must be careful as we read this text that we are not too quick to claim the language of persecution before we listen to and acknowledge the depth and reality of suffering for the name of Christ in our world. We must be mindful of how dangerous it is to be a Christian in some parts of today's world.

Excursus: The Name 'Christian'

Though for many today, 'Christian' is a badge of honour, the term may have originally been coined as a term of abuse by outsiders (as was the case, for example, with 'Methodist' and 'Quaker'). It only occurs three times in the whole New Testament (Acts 11.26; 26.28; 1 Peter 4.16), the followers of Jesus preferring other self-designations such as saints, disciples, the church of God, the way. Believers were apparently first called 'Christians' by pagan neighbours in Antioch.

Suffering 'as a Christian' therefore has connotations of name-calling, with the accompanying ridicule and hostility. 1 Peter presumes that pagans would put it on a par with suffering 'as a murderer' or 'as a mischief-maker' (4.15). In some places today, 'Christian' remains a derogatory term. But the early church turned this term of abuse upside down. Being reviled 'for the name of Christ' brings a blessing, as Christ himself promised in the Beatitudes (4.14; see also Matt. 5.11–12; Luke 6.22–23). The name Christian – someone related to, or defined by, Christ – now functions positively as an identity marker, giving his followers a positive identity.

Outsiders do not have a monopoly on name-calling, however. Christians have often resorted to derogatory names to denigrate the other, whether non-Christians or other members of the Christian family. The experience of our earliest co-religionists invites reflection on the ethics of name-calling.

As if coming full circle, this chapter returns not only to the suffering of Christ as the example for Christian suffering, but also to the reminder that God is a just judge who will ultimately sort things out. Jewish teachers often insisted that God punishes the righteous in this age to straighten them out, but he would punish the wicked in fuller measure in the day of judgement. In the Old Testament, God was sometimes stricter with his own people first, since they knew better (Jer. 25.29; Amos 3.2). God could begin judgement with his own house, his own sanctuary (Ezek. 9.6).

In 1 Peter, God's house is also God's household (2.5). Here, believers may experience unjust suffering as divine discipline in one sense (see Heb. 12.3–11), as something to make them better. But they could be assured that if even the righteous suffer, judgement will come far more harshly on those who disobey the gospel (4.17; see also Rom. 2.8). Again, Peter reminds his community that vindication will come, and that God will set all things right, a point which is reinforced in 4.17 and 4.18, with the latter quoting Proverbs 11.31. If God's own people suffer now, how much more can they expect God to punish the wicked?

Peter then concludes the chapter by drawing all of these themes together, encouraging those who are suffering for their faith to trust in God, who is faithful, and to continue to do good. In this final verse, Peter emphasizes God's will (2.15; 3.17; 4.19), including the idea of suffering being in accordance with God's will. In other words, those who suffer should not assume that they are outside God's will. God can use suffering in the lives of Peter's community as discipline to transform (4.17) or to bring others to glory, for example. Suffering then does not mean that a Christian is bad, or that one who suffers now is worse than someone who does not suffer now. Suffering according to God's will means that Peter's community can trust that God has a purpose in suffering, that suffering for Christ has meaning, even if wicked people (rather than God) are the ones directly causing it. This does not mean that they should seek suffering. But rather, Peter is encouraging those who are in a situation of suffering that they have not chosen. Suffering according to God's will in this context is suffering on account of one's devotion to Christ rather than for one's crimes or stupidity (4.15–16). Ultimately, they are to entrust themselves (literally 'their souls') to God, 'a faithful Creator'. Even while suffering, the foundation of their hope is in God who will not fail them. Because of this living hope, and because of God's faithfulness, they should not stop living, speaking, and serving; they must continue 'to do good'.

Questions for reflection

1 While suffering has been a focus throughout 1 Peter, it has been a particular focus of this fourth chapter.

 • What does it mean to suffer for being a Christian?

 • How can you ensure that suffering for Christ does not become an excuse to stop doing good and responding to injustice in your world?

 • How can you have joy in the midst of suffering?

 • Is all suffering redemptive? Why or why not?

2 1 Peter calls the Christian to mutual, genuine love and to hospitality.
  - Who are the strangers in your world?
  - What does it mean to 'love the stranger' in your context?
  - What is the cost of hospitality?

3 1 Peter is one of the few places where we find the word 'Christian'.
  - How do you respond to the reality that the name 'Christian' may have been coined as a term of abuse?
  - Is the term 'Christian' associated with shame and ridicule in your world? Is it a derogatory term?
  - How does 1 Peter reclaim the name 'Christian'?
  - What does being called 'Christian' mean in your context?

4 1 Peter speaks clearly about the hope that comes through Jesus' suffering and resurrection and the promised future glory for those who believe.
  - What does it mean to live in the resurrection power?

5

Authority in Christ
(1 Peter 5)

'Jesus, the good shepherd' (2014), Jyoti Sahi.

'Jesus, the good shepherd': the language of the shepherd and shepherding occurs across 1 Peter. Countless paintings of Jesus, the good shepherd, have been created all over the world. In this work, Jesus is not carrying a sheep, but watching over one that is separate from the rest of the flock, alienated from the flock. Perhaps it is suffering? Or is it the lost sheep that he searched for and found, contentedly sleeping, secure in the presence of Christ? Jesus' own face is weary, but he resolutely keeps his eyes open, so he can watch over the sleeping sheep and keep it safe. His is also a thoughtful face – what he is thinking we cannot know. But it is the face of one whom we, like the sheep, can trust to care for us even in the midst of alienation and suffering, to come and find us when we are lost, and to keep us safe. Jesus, in this way, models for us what it means to be a shepherd.

Jyoti Sahi, Indian artist and theologian, used by permission. https://indiaartsmovement.wordpress.com/2015/09/30/jyoti-sahi/

1 Peter 5 contains part of the letter's final teaching section. The section begins in 1 Peter 4.12 and continues to 1 Peter 5.11, connected by the word 'now' (literally 'therefore') at the start of chapter 5. In the midst of suffering just described in 1 Peter 4, chapter 5 makes clear that 'responsible leadership and unity in the congregation are especially vital' (Horrell 1998, p. 91). The chapter then concludes with greetings and a wish of peace from the apostolic author to those in the receiving community. While it is possible to focus on the first four verses of this chapter, verses that give a particular vision of Christian leadership, those verses must be understood both in the context of the chapter as a whole, and in the wider context of 1 Peter.

As we have just seen in 1 Peter 4, and across the whole of the letter, suffering marks the community to which Peter writes and the word 'suffer' occurs either as a noun or a verb some 16 times. In 15 of these times, the words 'suffer' or 'suffering' share the same root as the paschal sacrifice of Christ, thus linking the suffering of the community to Christ's experience of suffering (1.11; 2.19, 23; 3.14, 17–18; 4.1,13, 15, 19; 5.1, 9–10). As we read 1 Peter 5, then, we must keep the experience of suffering foremost in our minds, for all of the instructions in this chapter take place in the context of vulnerability and suffering, drawing on the exhortations in chapter 4.

In addition, 1 Peter is marked by love between the apostolic author and the recipients, who are called to 'love one another deeply from the heart' (1.22). Eight times in these five chapters, Peter uses either the verb or the noun 'love', often calling the hearers of the letter to act in loving ways towards one another (1.22; 2.17; 4.8; 5.14).

Finally, 1 Peter bears witness to God's care for and solidarity with God's creation, especially God's people, and to the ultimate promise of Christ's redemption upon his return (5.4, 6, 10). Thus, in spite of the presence of suffering, Peter also calls his community to hope in Christ's redemption of God's beloved world, and to reliance on the promise of God's care for God's creation.

1 Peter 5.1–4

[1] Now as an elder myself and a witness of the sufferings of Christ, as well as one who shares in the glory to be revealed, I exhort the elders among you [2] to tend the flock of God that is in your charge, exercising the oversight, not under compulsion but willingly, as God would have you do it – not for sordid gain but eagerly. [3] Do not lord it over those in your charge, but be examples to the flock. [4] And when the chief shepherd appears, you will win the crown of glory that never fades away.

These verses present an image of Christian leadership to the recipients of this letter. We have to remember that this letter was written before the solidifying of ministry into a three-fold order of bishop, presbyter and deacon. And unlike other New Testament writings, Peter does not use the term 'bishop' (*episkopos*) here although the words 'exercising the oversight' come from a related verb and are connected to the tending of the flock. Instead, 1 Peter prefers the term 'elder' which does not necessarily point to formal church leadership (see Acts 14.23; 1 Tim. 5; James 5.14). Rather, the term 'elder', which is a neutral term and can be translated as both female and male elders, designates people who are older within the congregation, and possibly people who are older in the faith.

In 5.1, Peter calls himself a 'fellow elder', rather than an apostle, teacher, or spiritual father. The choice is significant. In choosing the same title as those to whom he is writing, Peter signals his common cause with them. He writes to them as one of them, exhorting them as a fellow elder rather than commanding them as one in authority. Further, he speaks of the importance of bearing witness to the sufferings of Christ which, as in chapter 4, is immediately followed by mention of 'the glory to be revealed' (see 4.13; 1.10–12).

Peter exhorts the elders to shepherd the flock within their charge. This metaphor is grounded in the earth and in tending to the creatures of the earth. The verb 'to shepherd' echoes the command to Peter at the end of John's Gospel to shepherd and nurture the flock of Jesus (John 21.16). Moreover, it calls to mind Jesus' own teaching about the nature of the 'good shepherd' in John 10.1–18: the shepherd who lays down his life for the flock, whose sheep know his voice, who knows his sheep by name and who leads his sheep out to pasture. Moreover, the shepherd is also the one who searches for the lost sheep (Ezek. 34; Luke 15); the shepherd is both pastor and evangelist. This is a call to a demotion rather than a promotion within the ancient world.

Excursus: Shepherds

As a letter written to 'aliens and exiles', it is fitting that shepherds in the Roman world were considered outcasts; they were outsiders to the upper classes, as dirty, smelly people. A call to shepherd the flock of God thus must be a call to be with and among the people, to be involved with the most vulnerable of the community, a call away from status to service. For the author, the male and female elders must reflect this shepherding ethos. Moreover, in a reflection from a scholar who has served as a shepherd in her community, the shepherd leads from behind, allowing the flock to go where they want to go, giving them freedom and creativity. This shepherd is not in full control and does not know what kind of fruit or grass the sheep will prefer on any given day. The shepherd is responsible for keeping the flock together and protecting them so they can flourish in the pasture. The shepherd is not the commander of an army nor a general whose troops are to follow unquestioningly in step. The metaphor of shepherding for leadership contradicts a more domineering model such as might have been the case under the Roman imperial order.

Peter follows this call to 'tend the flock' with three ways that such shepherding should happen, focusing both on what this leadership should not entail and what it ought to look like. The shepherding is not to be done by compulsion, nor for gain, nor by lording it over those in their charge; rather, shepherding the flock is to be undertaken willingly, eagerly, and should set an example for the flock.

In the first set of negatives, Peter exhorts these elder shepherds against leading by compulsion or greed. Compulsion and greed reflect two sides of the same coin. In the first instance, a leader who leads not because she is willing but because she has no choice; in the second, a leader who leads not voluntarily but rather for what he can gain monetarily or by other means. In each case, compulsion and greed contradict the proper nature of an elder shepherd. Such a leader exhibits a free willingness to be a leader, neither suffering under duress nor seeking personal gain. Within the context of the persecuted church, such a leader would enter into leadership of the faith community knowing and accepting the risks, and not looking for personal glorification.

The exhortation in 5.3 continues Peter's image of elder leadership of the congregation. While implied in the metaphor of the shepherd – especially when literal shepherds so often lead from the back – the apostolic author explicitly forbids 'lording it over' the community. At the root of the Greek verb used here is the word 'lord'. The writer of 1 Peter seems to be reminding the elder leaders that they are not the lords of the community, for the community only has one Lord. Rather, they are to set an example. Implicit in this seems to be that the elders are to be examples of Jesus for the community, which does not surprise us in the context of this letter. Throughout 1 Peter, his hearers have been encouraged to imitate Christ in all aspects of their lives and to serve only Christ as Lord, not the many other competing lord-less powers (see 1 Peter 2 and 3). Now Peter takes the imitation of Christ one step further through the image of the shepherd, calling the elders to be examples to the flock of the good shepherd who both washes the feet of his disciples and challenges the injustice of the empire by laying down his life on behalf of his friends. The verb exhorting them to 'be examples' is better understood as 'becoming examples', which is active and a process, and this matters a great deal here. The elders are to work on becoming examples to the flock; they too must learn and grow to continue to be patterns for the rest of the believers. Like the living word, living hope, and living stones of 1 Peter, the elders cannot be stagnant in their shepherding. They should provide the way of life in the name of Christ that believers can imitate.

Additionally, the word here translated as 'those in your charge' has the same root as the word 'inherit-ance', or 'the portion you inherit'. Shepherds, thus, receive a portion over which they are to exercise pastoral oversight. The portion is not theirs to choose, but rather their allotment. Shepherds must attend to the entire portion under their care, which cannot simply be the persons within their community but the entire created order that falls under their care, especially those parts of their allotment that are in crisis. We remember here the exhortations throughout 1 Peter that are directed to 'all' and not just a certain part of the community. As in the Lukan parable of the lost sheep (Luke 15), shepherds retain responsibility not only for the 99 but also for the one.

The elders, women and men, are reminded in 5.4 that they too remain members of the flock, that they too are shepherded by 'the chief shepherd'. The 'elders' are not the chief shepherd. No one called to be shepherd in this world is the chief shepherd as that role is only for God in Christ. Thus, the elders stand in a liminal space: they are both sheep and shepherd, both needing guidance and called to guide. The promise here is that of a crown of glory, a reward for their faithfulness. This promise is quite tricky, because the purpose of the crown of glory is not to encourage greed or lording over. Instead, in this crown lies an implicit critique of the world order, reminiscent of the challenges to power beneath 1 Peter 2.11–3.7 (see also 1.6–7). Once again, we find the language of glory, a glory that 'never fades away'. Unlike the crowns of this world, which represent the lords of this world, often made of metals or even of greenery and flowers, this crown of glory will not fade or perish. Here we cannot forget the promise in 1.4 of an inheritance that is 'imperishable' and 'unfading'. The promise to those who follow Christ is not one of perishable glory in this world, but of glory that never fades when Christ, the good shepherd, appears.

---

1 Peter 5.5–11

[5] In the same way, you who are younger must accept the authority of the elders. And all of you must clothe yourselves with humility in your dealings with one another, for 'God opposes the proud, but gives grace to the humble.' [6] Humble yourselves therefore under the mighty hand of God, so that he may exalt you in due time. [7] Cast all your anxiety on him, because he cares for you. [8] Discipline yourselves, keep alert. Like a roaring lion your adversary the devil prowls around, looking for someone to devour. [9] Resist him, steadfast in your faith, for you know that your brothers and sisters in all the world are undergoing the same kinds of suffering. [10] And after you have suffered for a little while, the God of all grace, who has called you to his eternal glory in Christ, will himself restore, support, strengthen, and establish you. [11] To him be the power forever and ever. Amen.

This second section of teaching in 1 Peter 5 turns its attention to the entire community – to 'all of you' – of which the elders are a part. With the exception of the first half of 5.5 to 'accept the authority of the elders' (here we immediately think of the repetitions of this command in chapters 2–3), these verses apply equally to elders as to the rest of the community. Thus, while it would be perfectly acceptable to focus merely on 5.1–4 as instructions for Christian leadership, this latter section also has much to teach concerning what it might mean to be a person called to shepherd God's flock.

In interpreting the opening statement in 5.5, a danger lurks and we must think back to the lengthy discussion of submission and 'accepting authority' in 2.13–3.7. It is all too easy to get caught up in being called as an elder and to understand leadership not in solidarity with the flock but only in terms of power. For such a pithy statement as 5.5, as we now know, could easily become a bludgeon, here to silence younger or newer members of the community: 'you who are younger'. As a result, the beginning of 5.5 must be read as a response to elders just described: those who model themselves after the good shepherd, serving without compulsion or greed, and who do not lord their position over the rest of the community. We are to remember from earlier in this letter that there is only one Lord and that that Lord is Jesus Christ and not the elders. To elders like those described in 5.1–4, younger members could safely submit themselves; without such elders in place, submission could lead to abuse of power and systems of oppression about which Peter has already offered counsel.

From 5.5 to 5.11, 1 Peter turns to the theme of humility as a characteristic of the entire community, including elders and younger members, and one that changes the face of power. Even though there is a structure of authority in the church and even in the home, 'humility should characterize all members of the congregation' (Horrell 1998, p. 94). An important distinction needs to be made about the word 'humility' in 5.5. Here, the Greek word is one that can also mean 'modesty' rather than the word that Mary uses in the Magnificat ('the lowliness of his servant'; Luke 1.48), where we find in Luke a word better translated as humiliation. From 1 Peter 5.5, the community of faith is called to mutual modesty with one another, whether elder or younger. This should not be interpreted as biblical justification of the humiliation of some (younger) members of the community by others. Perhaps, drawing from the Latin word of 'humility', another way to put this is that the community is called to be grounded, each thinking of her or himself soberly and not more importantly than he or she is. Moreover, Peter underscores his call to humility by reminding the community of the scriptures' counsel that 'God opposes the proud but gives grace to the humble' (see Prov. 3.34; and also James 4.6).

Verses 6–7 of chapter 5 should be read together, as they are one sentence in Greek. To begin, one notices a distinction between 5.6 and the second part of 5.5. The earlier verse called for humility, or modesty, towards one another. It is worth noting here that within the context of persecution and suffering, humility or modesty is a strategy of survival rather than a method of attaining piety (see also the discussion on survival in Chapters 2 and 3). However, 5.6 shifts the discourse from relationships between community members to the call of the whole community to take its correct posture before God. Here the elders stand in exactly the same relationship to God as the younger members of the faith. Before God, all are humbled; no one is exalted, except by God's own actions. Moreover, God's uplifting of the humble reflects God's nature; it is not a prize meted out to the most humble within the community. Humility is not a competition. Here, reading 5.5 and 5.6 together, Peter's exhortation to humility echoes the teaching of Jesus in the Gospels: 'all who exalt themselves will be humbled, and all who humble themselves will be exalted' (Matt. 23.12).

Peter then immediately connects humility with the casting off of anxiety. While the NRSV translation above reads 'cast all your anxiety on him', a more accurate translation is 'casting all your anxieties on him'. That is, casting one's anxieties on God is part of the act of humbling oneself before God.

A person who gives their anxieties to God reflects their posture towards God. To live humbly under 'the mighty hand of God' is to entrust oneself, one's suffering and one's cares to God. Here too we find Peter grounded in the tradition of Scripture and of Jesus, where in the Psalms God's people are told to 'Cast your burden on the LORD, and he will sustain you' (55.22) and Jesus tells his followers not to 'worry about your life' (Matt. 6.25–34). This is a reminder to elders and to the entire flock of who is in charge, a reminder of the Christ who promised rest to those who were burdened (Matt. 11.27–28). Read together, 5.6–7 call elders and all of God's flock to take their appropriate place before God, the God who cares for all the faithful just as God cares for the 'birds of the air' (Matt. 6.26). Peter doesn't say that those who follow Christ will never have anxiety or worry. Suffering is assumed for those who follow Christ in Peter's communities. But Peter does assure his readers that they can trust in God and God's promises – they can cast this anxiety onto him and humble themselves under his hand – because God's love and care endure.

Having assumed their proper posture towards God, Peter then reminds all Christians of their proper posture towards their 'adversary, the devil' which is a posture of watchful, sober-minded resistance. The word translated as 'keep alert' should have a familiar ring, as Jesus frequently demands this of the disciples (see Matt. 24.42–43;

25.13; 26.38, 40–41; Mark 13.34–35, 37; 14.34, 37–38; Luke 12.37). Paul, like Peter, pairs the command to 'keep alert', with the command to be sober-minded, translated here as 'discipline your-selves' (see 1 Thess. 5.6). These actions, of course, invert the actions of the disciples in the garden of Gethsemane on the night of Jesus' arrest. Rather than following their example and falling asleep, the elders and members of this community are charged to be alert and sober-minded, ready to resist the adversary. As a leader, a shepherd, the text does not offer an option for laziness but is clear that part of being a good shepherd is resisting the adversary, described vividly as a roaring lion.

The word 'adversary' in 5.8 derives from courts of law in the Roman world. The 'adversary' in this instance functioned as the accusing or prosecuting attorney, charging those on trial with crimes against the state or the emperor. The Gospel of Matthew records this sort of persecutory behaviour against Christians (5.25–26), as does James (2.6–7). However, one must also keep in mind the executions by wild beasts already taking place in the Roman arenas, replete with roaring lions. All of these images come into play in 1 Peter 5.8. Each of these metaphors underscores that the adversary is not a 'person' per se, but a maleficent force, larger than any member of Peter's community. Peter charges all Christians to resist these diabolical forces in 5.9. Here, there are echoes of David, the young shepherd, reminding

King Saul that he resists lions for a living (1 Sam. 17.32–37).

For contemporary Christians in the global church, those forces that stand for all that is evil are numerous and should be named. At times it is easier to tell those who are suffering to keep quiet and to endure their suffering – the problematic elements of these responses we have already explored in Chapters 2 and 3 – but Jesus' radical call in this final chapter of 1 Peter is to confront the lions, to resist the adversary, to protect the flock.

Excursus: Dangers in the Pasture

Within 1 Peter 5, the language of the roaring lion and adversary cannot be detached from the language of tending the flock. Certainly, Peter exhorts 'all of you' to resist the adversary, standing steadfast in faith. But those who are responsible for tending the flock of God must also be aware of the dangers in the pasture. How do we name the lions that are in the pastures where the flock is grazing? How easy is it to ignore the lion rather than confront it as it snatches away sheep? 1 Peter 5 exhorts all to oppose the lion, steadfast in faith. Part of being a good shepherd, therefore, means resisting the lion.

It is worth noting that 1 Peter balances the call to resilience for those who are vulnerable and marginalized with the call to resistance for those in positions of power and authority (such as those who are called to shepherd). For some, resilience is the right response to a situation of suffering, for others, resistance is the best way forward. The letter highlights both responses to suffering and oppression but doesn't command either as the only way in every situation. In our world today, we need to take care not to imply that there is one right way to respond to suffering. The testimony of those in the midst of suffering is almost always different from those observing from the outside.

An important clause at the end of 5.9 reminds the community that they do not face persecution alone. Instead, they face what their siblings in the faith have or are facing in other parts of the Roman empire. Peter reminds his community of their solidarity one with another, not unlike the metaphor of the body found in 1 Corinthians 12. Their unity in Christ overcomes all division and threat, even as they suffer. They do not suffer alone, nor do they resist alone. They are joined in both of these by their global brothers and sisters in the faith, a helpful reminder to the twenty-first-century church as well.

The passage ends by returning once again to the central themes of hope, suffering and glory in Christ. 'After you have suffered for a little while' echoes the first reference to suffering 'for a short time' in 1.6. And here, as there, Peter speaks of God's promise for divine restoration 'to his eternal glory in Christ' (5.10). The temporary nature of the suffering – for a little while, for a short time – is set against the everlasting promise of salvation. At the end of the letter, the promise of what salvation entails is specific: called to 'eternal glory in Christ', God will 'restore, support, strengthen, and establish you' (5.10). This is the God who takes on anxiety, this is the God in whom Peter's followers must trust, and this is the God to whom 'be power for ever and ever' (5.11). The power of God has the final word for whatever suffering is endured for Christ; God's promises revealed in Christ are firm.

The ending rings with certainty, but leaves little space for lament and for the experience of divine silence. Peter seems certain that the troubles of his community will end in due time, by divine intervention. Importantly, God and not the elders who shepherd the community, will bring about restoration. All must wait on God, and God's strengthening power.

> ## 1 Peter 5.12–14
>
> [12] Through Silvanus, whom I consider a faithful brother, I have written this short letter to encourage you and to testify that this is the true grace of God. Stand fast in it. [13] Your sister church in Babylon, chosen together with you, sends you greetings; and so does my son Mark. [14] Greet one another with a kiss of love. Peace to all of you who are in Christ.

The letter ends with greetings, as is customary; however, the greetings continue the theme of the entire letter. In 5.12, Peter underscores the truth of the grace of God and encourages the community to stand in that grace. For a community under siege, and for the elders who shepherd them, this serves as another reminder that even in the midst of persecution the community of faith stands, and rests in God's grace. Issuing the reminder of the presence of God's grace falls not only to Peter, but also to all who shepherd the community. All are called to testify to the grace of God, just as all are to be prepared to testify to the hope that is in them (3.15–16).

Excursus: The Co-elect in Babylon

The translation of 5.13 in the NRSV (above) misses the mark. Nowhere in the Greek words of this passage does the phrase 'church' occur. Instead, we find the feminine words 'the co-elect one' which could literally translate as 'She who is co-elect with you in Babylon'. This feminine one 'who is co-elect' need not be a church, especially when paired with Mark, who is clearly a person. Instead, the greeter may be one of several women from the church in Rome (which Peter calls 'Babylon') that Paul greets in Romans 16, or some other female church leader known to the community and co-elect with them. This possible presence of female church leaders even in the earliest church, not unlike those leaders addressed in Paul's letters to Rome and Corinth, is a reminder of God's ability to call all persons to God's service regardless of gender.

Nevertheless, for some, the reality that 'church' is feminine in the Greek justifies the addition of this word to 1 Peter 5.13 and numerous ancient scribes read 1 Peter this way. However, the language of 'co-elect' is significant and missed in such a translation. For 'co-elect' brings us at the very end of 1 Peter back to the beginning, emphasizing the chosen status of God's people who were not a people, but are now God's people (1.1–2; 2.9–10).

Babylon here, as mentioned at the start of this commentary, is almost certainly Rome and some manuscripts of 1 Peter actually have the word 'Rome' here instead of Babylon (Horrell 1998, p. 101; see also Rev. 17.5). Babylon was the place where the Jews were in exile according to Daniel, and thus ties in well with Peter's recipients who are also 'exiles and aliens'. Such language, therefore, confirms the dominant and oppressive power of the empire in which God's chosen people are scattered that we find throughout this letter.

Peter then calls his recipients to greet one another with a loving kiss. For some, kissing once or multiple times is a commonplace greeting. For others, it represents a decided breach of etiquette or boundaries. Peter does not intend to shock here, but to call the community to physical, visible, warm expressions of care and love for one another, which may look different in different communities. The emphases in these final parts of the letter are on relationship, reconciliation and resisting all that seeks to divide and kill our call to be one in Christ. For when a community is no longer made up of brothers and sisters in relationship with one another and sharing the kiss of peace, issues and divisions inevitably arise.

Peter ends with an expression of peace 'to all of you who are in Christ'. In our fractured denominational world, such an expression challenges the contemporary church to consider what actions it takes and will take to increase peace within each community, tradition, and communion of Christ's church. Both the peace and the love that Peter expresses occur in a time of persecution for the Church, at a time when the community of 1 Peter is suffering. This challenges the contemporary church to wonder what such peace and love might look like for us today in the global church as we follow Christ and seek to imitate him in his suffering and sacrificial love.

Read as a whole, then, 1 Peter 5.1–14 gives a broader and deeper vision of church leadership than can be gleaned from the first four verses alone. For 1 Peter, leadership involves more than the command that women and men, elders of the community, should shepherd the sheep free of compulsion, greed, or self-aggrandizement. Such leaders should also exercise humility towards all other members of the community, and take their rightful, humble place before the God who cares for all of them. In addition, such leaders must remain sober-minded and awake, watching and listening for the roaring lion that threatens to devour; and with their community, they are to resist this diabolical lion, standing strong in their faith. However, such leaders are not alone; for God will support and strengthen them and the hope of eternal glory in Christ sustains them. Moreover, they suffer alongside their brothers and sisters around the world, and God cares and will intervene on their behalf. Finally such leaders are reminded that God's grace is true; and they are called to acts of love and expressions of peace, especially among God's people. Even in situations of suffering and persecution, reconciliation in love and the peace of Christ may prevail.

Questions for reflection

1 Peter speaks of the qualities of an elder who shepherds God's flock, nurturing the community of faith with which they are entrusted.
   • How do you understand a shepherd in your culture?
   • What are the characteristics of a Christ-like leader?
   • Who has been a Christ-like leader in your life? Why?

2 Peter speaks of the importance of bearing witness to the sufferings of Christ, not simply Christ's future glorification.
   • How do we bear witness to the sufferings of Christ today?
   • Where do we see Christ's sufferings?

3 1 Peter promises those who are faithful a crown of glory.

- What does glory look like to shepherds and sheep in different circumstances?
- How is speaking about glory to a persecuted church different from speaking about glory to a church that has power and is living in peaceful times?
- How does this crown of glory differ from the crown that would have been worn by the emperor?

4 1 Peter warns the community of faith against the 'roaring lion, seeking to devour'.

- Who are the roaring lions that prowl about in your world?
- How have you seen evil affect your community?
- Given the presence of roaring lions what, then, is the charge of those elder women and men who shepherd parts of God's flock?
- What might resistance look like in each of their contexts?
- And how, in the midst of this, do they keep steadfast in their faith?
- How do you balance the call to be resilient (chapter 2–3) and to resist (chapter 5)?

Bibliography and Further Reading

Achtemeier, Paul J., 1996, *1 Peter: A Commentary on First Peter*, Hermeneia. Minneapolis: Fortress Press.

Bartlett, David L., 2003, 'The First Letter of Peter: Introduction, Commentary, and Reflections', in L. E. Keck (ed.), *The New Interpreter's Bible*, vol. 12, Nashville: Abingdon Press, 229–319.

Bird, Jennifer G., 2011, *Abuse, Power and Fearful Obedience: Reconsidering 1 Peter's Commands to Women*, New York: T&T Clark.

Bockmuehl, Markus, 2012a, 'Hope and Optimism in Straitened Times', *Pro Ecclesia* 21(1): 7–24, http://www.e-ccet.org/wp/wp-content/uploads/2012/03/Bockmuehl_Commentary2.pdf (accessed 28 September 2019).

Bockmuehl, Markus, 2012b, *Simon Peter in Scripture and Memory: The New Testament Apostle in the Early Church*, Grand Rapids: Baker Academic.

Boring, Eugene M., 1999, *1 Peter*, Abingdon New Testament Commentaries, Nashville: Abingdon Press.

Cervantes Gabarrón, José, 1991, 'El pastor en la teología de 1 Pe', *Estudios biblicos* 49: 331–51.

Cipriani, S., 1990, '"Evangelizzazione" e "Missione" nella prima lettera di Pietro', *Richerche storico bibliche* 2: 125–38.

Clowney, Edmund, 1988, *The Message of 1 Peter: The Way of the Cross*, The Bible Speaks Today, Downers Grove, IL: InterVarsity Press.

Dijkman, J. H. L., 1986, 'ὅτι as an introductory formula to catechetical references in 1 Peter', in J. H. Petzer and P. J. Hartin (eds), *A South African Perspective on the New Testament*, Leiden: Brill, 260–70.

Elliott, John H., 1990, *A Home for the Homeless: A Social-Scientific Criticism of I Peter, Its Situation and Strategy*, Philadelphia: Fortress Press.

Elliott, John H., 1992, 'First Epistle of Peter', in *Anchor Bible Dictionary*, vol. V, New York: Doubleday, 269–78.

Elliott, John H., 2000, *1 Peter*, Anchor Bible 37B, London: Yale University Press.

Elliott, John H., 2008, 'Elders as Leaders in 1 Peter and the early Church', *HTS Teologiese Studies* 64(2): 681–95.

Fuller, Matt, 2017, *Perfect Sinners: See Yourself as God Sees You*, Epsom: The Good Book Company.

Goppelt, Leonhard, 1993, *A Commentary on 1 Peter*, trans. J. E. Alsup, Grand Rapids: Eerdmans.

Grudem, Wayne, 1994, *Systematic Theology*, Grand Rapids: Zondervan.

Harink, Douglas, 2009, *1 & 2 Peter*, Theological Commentary on the Bible series, London: SCM Press.

The HarperCollins Bible Dictionary, 1996, Paul J. Achtemeier (ed.), Nashville: HarperCollins Publishers.

Horrell, David G., 1998, *The Epistles of Peter and Jude*, Epworth Commentaries, Peterborough: Epworth Press.

Horrell, David G., 2008, *1 Peter*, New Testament Guides, London: T&T Clark.

Jobes, Karen H., 2005, *1 Peter*, Grand Rapids: Baker Academic.

Johnson, Luke Timothy, 2010, *The Writings of the New Testament: An Interpretation*, Minneapolis: Fortress Press.

Kayalaparampil, Thomas, 1989, 'Christian People, A Royal Priesthood (A Study on 1 Peter 2:9)', *Bible-hashyam* 15: 154–69.

Keener, Craig S., 2013, *Acts: An Exegetical Commentary, 3:1–14:28*, Grand Rapids: Baker Academic.

Keener, Craig S., 2014, *The IVP Bible Background Commentary: New Testament*, Downers Grove, Ill: IVP Academic.

Rodríguez, Raúl Lugo, 1996, 'Forasteros y emigrantes (1 Pe. 2,11): Reflexión biblica sobre la naturaleza de los cristianos en cuanto peregrinos', *QOL* 11: 35–45.

Perkins, Pheme, 1995, *First and Second Peter, James, and Jude*, Interpretation Bible Commentary, Louisville, KY: John Knox Press.

Powell, Mark Allen, 1998, *Introduction to the Gospels*, Minneapolis, Fortress Press.

Schreiner, Thomas R., 2003, *1, 2 Peter, Jude*, The New American Commentary 37, Nashville: Broadman & Holman Publishers.

Schüssler Fiorenza, Elizabeth, 2007, 'The First Letter of Peter', in Fernando F. Segovia and R. S. Sugirtharajah (eds), *A Postcolonial Commentary of the New Testament Writings*, London: T&T Clark, 380–403.

Setzer, Claudia, 2011, 'The First Letter of Peter', in Amy Jill Levine and Marc Zvi Brettler (eds), *The Jewish Annotated New Testament*, New York: Oxford University Press, 436–42.

Smith, Shively T. J., 2016, *Strangers to Family: Diaspora and 1 Peter's Invention of God*, Waco, TX: Baylor University Press.

Spencer, John R., 1992, 'Sojourner', in *Anchor Bible Dictionary*, vol. 6, New York: Doubleday, 103–4.

Volf, Miroslav, 1994, 'Soft Difference: Theological Reflections on the Relation between Church and Culture in 1 Peter', *Ex auditu* 10: 15–30.

Index of Bible References

Index of Names and Subjects

INDEX OF NAMES AND SUBJECTS